Special Foods for Special Kids

Practical Solutions & Great Recipes
for Children with FOOD ALLERGIES

☆ Todd Adelman & Jodi Behrend ☆

Robert D. Reed Publishers
San Francisco

Cover design by Robin Schneider

Robert D. Reed Publishers
San Francisco

ISBN 1-885003-38-2
Library of Congress Catalog Card No. 99-067838

For Dad - You believed it's never what we've been "taught" that's important, but what we've "learned." From you I learned that experimentation plays an important role in experience. You spent your life trying to make the path a little easier for children. I learned from that too.
Together we're still flying kites.......and dreaming!

Todd

For Mom - You've spent a lifetime believing in me. Thank you for your unconditional love, support and sense of humor. You taught me early on, there's more to life than greasing a pan. "I really appreciate it" and remain your biggest fan.

Jodi

Acknowledgments

The concept for Special Foods for Special Kids was the result of a casual dinner conversation about where we were going in our careers. How could we combine our professional and personal experiences to help acknowledge a subject that has not been fully addressed...cooking for children with food allergies? Co-writing a cookbook for parents of these children seemed to be the perfect solution.

This book has been four years in the making and has come together with the help and support from many sources. Family, friends and colleagues have provided on-going encouragement, constructive criticism and support. It's hard to imagine being asked to taste 14 different versions of the same chocolate cake recipe and still be upbeat!

Special thanks to:
Diane & Eyal for their love and support.
Jodi's Dad for his invaluable advice.
Todd's Mom for her unending faith.
Emily for being an inspiration.
Brooklyn School for Special Children & Sandy for allowing us to test recipes and encouraging us to go forward with this project.
Our Recipe Testers Group for all of your hard work and the families who shared their personal experiences with us.
All of the children who taste tested recipes and offered their opinions - good or bad!
Heidi for her professional expertise.

We are also grateful to the companies who graciously donated their products enabling us to create "kid friendly" allergy-free dishes:

Ener-G Foods
Arrowhead Mills
Natural Food Technologies
LifeSource Natural Foods, Inc.
Pamela's Products, Inc.

Wholesome & Hearty Foods
Imagine Foods
American Natural Snacks
GoLightly Chocolate
Miss Roben's Gluten-Free Products

Extra special thanks to Robin for bringing life to our pages and enhancing their character.

And to all of those people who constantly asked, "Are you done with that book yet?"
....The answer is finally......YES!

Contents

This cookbook is designed to help parents who have children with food allergies. Our intention is to provide "kid friendly" recipes with appropriate ingredient substitutions.   There is no substitution for medical guidance. Children under medical care for food allergies should consult with their physicians before making any changes to their diets. The reader accepts sole responsibility for the use of the information contained in this book.

Foreword

The primary focus in Pediatrics is no longer infectious disease. Emerging concerns such as developmental issues account for more than forty percent of office visits (1). The interest has apparently shifted to wellness issues and among the most common problems, we find nutrition and food allergies. This change in concerns can be explained not only because we are a more health conscious public but also due to the increasing number of food associated problems. It is reflected in the number of allergy triggered respiratory illnesses being diagnosed. Evidence of this is seen in the number of hospital emergency room and office visits for the evaluation of allergy symptoms (2). Indirectly, the expanding availability of new pharmaceuticals to treat allergy symptoms also indicates the prevalence of this emerging public health concern.

This new direction requires that we be familiar with the signs and symptoms of food allergies and heed their warnings, because repeated exposure to these agents could potentially lead to anaphylaxis- a true emergency. The focus of therapy includes identifying the responsible agent and eliminating it from the diet. This is an easy task if the only item the child is sensitive to happens to be Kiwi. But, what happens if it is the casein protein in dairy? It requires the appreciation that eliminating milk is not the only intervention, and the mindfulness to identify all food items that might contain casein as an ingredient. This becomes somewhat more complicated.

Special Foods for Special Kids offers a practical guide. It provides nutritional solutions with a variety of child- friendly foods. The useful section on acceptable substitutions enables parents to plan a balanced diet. The Resource Directory provides comprehensive information for obtaining products not readily found in your local grocery store.

Our group practice has decided to purchase several copies of this valuable book to address the often asked, "What can I give him for lunch?"

Clifford Mevs, MD, FAAP
Clinical Assistant Professor of Pediatrics
NYU School of Medicine

Footnotes:
1. Richmond, J. & Janis, J.M. : Ripeness is All The Coming of Age of Behavioral Pediatrics; Levine, M.D. ;
     Carey, W.B. ; Crocker, A.C. et. al (editors) Developemental - Behavioral Pediatrics, Philadelphia, W. B. Saunders, 1983

2. Synopsis Book, Best Articles Relevant to Pediatric Allergy and Immunology, Pediatrics (supplement),
    August 1999, Vol. 104, Number 2.

Chapter 1

What do you mean my child has a food allergy?

Our daughter, Emily, was eating dinner when she suddenly began to have problems breathing. She wasn't choking on a piece of food; her throat seemed to be closing up. We panicked. What was going on? At the hospital, they gave her an injection and informed us that she had had an allergic reaction to something she had eaten. We went over the list a dozen times. What food was it? Would she ever eat normally again? We took her to an allergist and, after several weeks of testing, we discovered she was allergic to several foods, including eggs, which are in so many things we eat. What about cake?...Mayonnaise?...Emily loves pancakes. We were frightened of every food she tasted and concerned about depriving her of the foods that she loves.

Kids and Food Allergies

Emily is one of the 30 to 40 million Americans who have some type of allergic condition. According to an American Medical Association survey, 8 percent of all children under the age of 6 have food allergies. Ninety-five percent of children's allergies are to milk, eggs, wheat, soybeans, seafood, nuts and peanuts (which are legumes).

Studies have shown allergic tendencies are inherited. If one parent has an allergy, there is a 30 to 35 percent chance of the child developing an allergy. When both parents are allergic, there is a 50 to 60 percent chance each of their children will be allergic as well. Even if neither parent is allergic, there still remains a 10 percent chance the child will inherit allergic tendencies.

It is important that parents recognize both the signs and symptoms of food allergies, as well as their child's specific needs. Allergic reactions can range from minimal (runny nose) to severe (anaphylactic shock).

SYMPTOMS INDICATING A FOOD ALLERGY

Diarrhea	Hives	Coughing	Headaches
Swelling	Rashes	Vomiting	Irritability
Colic	Shock	Wheezing	Runny/stuffy Nose

If one or more of these symptoms occurs every time your child eats a certain food, consult your pediatrician.

Parents should feel comfortable learning the difference between a possible allergic reaction and the signs and symptoms of another type of medical condition or disability. For example, parents who have children with a swallowing disorder or a sensory integration problem (where children cannot tolerate certain food textures) should not mistake their child's rejection of a particular food as a true food allergy. By the same token, very young children and children who are unable to communicate verbally may, in fact, be experiencing a true allergic reaction but are unable to let you know. Discussion with your child's pediatrician will help clarify the stages of your child's growth and development.

Food allergies are unique to the individual. Some children may outgrow them, while others may not. Certain food allergies may improve with repeated, small exposures, supervised by a doctor. Other allergies, like most allergies to nuts, tend to worsen over time and can lead to anaphylaxis. Close consultation with your child's pediatrician and/or allergist will help you plan for what is yet to come.

Coping with a Food Allergy

For some of us, avoiding a particular food may be easy. Certain foods, such as shrimp or peanut butter can be readily identified and omitted from our diet. If your child is allergic to dairy products, eggs or gluten, however, planning meals and buying and preparing food can be a nightmare.

At Zack's weekly playgroup, my neighbor Helen decided to have all of the kids make holiday cookies. The kids loved the idea. She is usually very careful to have something special for my son. He's allergic to milk and eggs. When I went to pick him up, Zack proudly showed me his bag of cookies and said, "Mommy, everyone can eat these, even me!" Helen explained that she used a prepackaged mix that didn't need milk or eggs added. I thought that was great, so I asked to see the box. Sure enough...dried milk was an ingredient in the mix. I can't forget the expression on Zack's face as I tried explaining he really couldn't eat the cookies. Helen meant well. EVERYONE felt awful!

So many of a child's "favorite" foods (cookies, cakes, pasta, ice cream) contain hidden ingredients. Allergens are frequently disguised under different names, making meal times a difficult task.

Helen was sensitive enough to try to make Zack feel like part of the group. If she had only called Zack's mother ahead of time, both parents could have carefully read the food labels, checking for any hidden ingredients. In fact, it would be a good idea if every parent in the playgroup were aware of Zack's food restrictions. Providing a list of alternative ingredients would also be helpful.

> *As an administrator of a child care program I try to educate staff to be extra cautious regarding the children's dietary needs. One day, I went into a classroom to observe breakfast. I happened to know that one of the students is allergic to milk. The staff were very careful to make sure this child was served juice instead of milk, but there in front of this little boy, was a bagel with cream cheese! It never crossed their minds to associate cheese with milk. The result of such a mistake could have been disastrous.*

Who would have thought that vanilla extract contains gluten? Does the average person remember that mayonnaise contains eggs; and that dairy includes milk, butter, cream and cheese? How often do we pay attention to the possibility that some of the ingredients in cake and bread may be dairy products, eggs and gluten? Are you aware that egg substitutes can include eggs and some non-dairy creamers contain dairy? For those of us with severe food allergies, the slightest amount of an offending allergen can trigger a reaction. Just "a little bit" can lead to a trip to the hospital.

Faced with the prospect that your child could become seriously ill from something you feed him, who wouldn't be scared of every mouthful? This is a very normal reaction. As hard as it is for you, it is important not to panic. Your child could be facing this allergy for the rest of his life. The impact of this is enormous. No one has done anything wrong or is to blame.

It is important that both you and your child understand this. You are the one who knows him best. He is depending on you to help him comprehend what having a food allergy means. Listen to his concerns. Watch what happens whenever he has an allergic reaction and begin to explain the adjustments that may lie ahead. Remember, this is an ongoing process that should continue until your child has a very clear understanding of what his dietary restrictions are.

Finding Solutions

The first thing to remember is that what seems like an insurmountable problem can be handled. As you begin helping your child to cope, try not to be overly cautious. Leaving the controlled environment your home provides may make you feel uneasy. But overreacting may cause your child to suffer socially as well as nutritionally. Going to school, eating out, sleepovers, parties and even time at Grandma's house are all important parts of your child's social development. Learn to ask questions about food preparation. This is no time to be shy. Familiarize yourself with ingredient labels. Shopping for your family may seem overwhelming, but you can take control over the kinds of food and ingredients your child will eat.

Start by finding out everything you can about your child's allergy signs and symptoms. Share this information with your child's teacher or day care provider. Parents should be aware that the United States Department of Agriculture (USDA) mandates all schools and day care centers that participate in the National School Breakfast and Lunch Programs provide "appropriate meals to children with medically certified special dietary needs." Ask for the school menu in advance so food alternatives can be discussed and provided. Develop a plan, together with the school, in the event your child has an allergic reaction. *What will the symptoms be? What actions should be taken? Who has the medication? Who should be called?* Encourage the school's staff to join you in taking an active role on behalf of your child.

The impossible will become possible with careful planning and investigation.

What about birthday cake?...Milk and cookies?...Pizza?...Ice cream?
Old family recipes may need to be adapted. New recipes will have to be found. With some research, creativity and experimentation using comparable substitutes, your child should be able to enjoy many of his favorite foods. Frozen fruit pops are just as much of a treat as ice cream and a tasty birthday cake can be made using gluten-free flours. Remember, your child's emotional well being is equally as important as his physical health. Anyone who is involved in your child's daily routine plays an important role. Your entire family will be undergoing changes. Everyone must come to grips with what those changes are and how they will be faced. Get everyone in on the act - siblings, grandparents, baby-sitters, teachers...everyone!

Communication is the Key

★ Observe your child and listen to his concerns
★ Talk with your pediatrician
★ Plan a consultation with a pediatric allergist
★ Meet with your child's teacher/day care provider, school nurse and cafeteria staff
★ Visit your local library and bookstore
★ Contact the Food Allergy Network (800-929-4040), a national non-profit organization that provides parents with information about children and food allergies
★ Surf the Internet for chat rooms, message boards and web sites

I hate Halloween!!! Every year, my friends and I go trick -or- treating and they fight over who gets the most candy. I'm not allowed to eat it. They eat the stuff for weeks and I have to listen to how great everything tastes. My parents make me give all of my candy to my brother. This makes me feel really bad. I know I'm not supposed to eat bread because it has something called "gluten" in it. Why can't I eat my candy?

In this situation, these parents are more than familiar with the hidden gluten found in candy. They have learned to carefully read food labels. This information needs to be relayed to their child. It is important he understand what he can and cannot eat and why. A good idea would be to prearrange your trick or treating. Offer some non-food items, such as stickers and small toys, at your own house. Speak to your neighbors to suggest having some of the same at their homes as well.

Special events should become more of a social activity and focus less on food. Help everyone become comfortable with the necessary adjustments that need to be made. Plan ahead for meal times outside of your home, offering food alternatives or substitutions, particularly for occasions where eating is going to be an issue. Remember, for your child, being like everyone probably seems more important than eating safe foods. This ongoing communication will be instrumental in helping to ensure your child feels like "one of the crowd."

How do I tell my child he has a food allergy?
It's time to have a talk with your child. Prepare yourself by finding a comfortable place and time for both of you. This conversation is about spending quality time to help your child understand what is going on. It's important that he participate. Elicit feedback by asking questions. Remind him of the symptoms he experiences whenever he eats certain foods and ask how that makes him feel. Try to think of circumstances when this routinely happens (snack time at school, eating Sunday breakfast, etc.).

Explain that the reason all of this is happening to him is because he is allergic to certain foods. Depending on your child's age, your description of what this actually means will be different. For a preschooler, it may be as simple as saying "You know that when you eat pizza it makes your stomach hurt." For an older child, a more detailed explanation of what an allergy is may be in order. It's important to reach your child at his level. One thing that can be particularly helpful for children of all ages is to relate their experiences to anyone they already know who has an allergy or is on a special diet. Your child will feel better just knowing "Uncle Mike is in the same boat."

Discuss what can be done to prevent triggering an allergic reaction. Avoiding the offending food is obviously the best way. Identify situations that could be a problem and talk about solutions together. Encourage your child to ask questions about ingredients and food preparation. Even at an early age, he should learn to be responsible for knowing that he cannot eat ice cream because it contains dairy.

There are a variety of ways to help you and your child feel confident about making suitable food choices. Some suggestions include:

* Make a chart by cutting out pictures of foods your child can and cannot eat
* Plan a trip to the supermarket and health food store - include teaching your child how to read food labels
* Ask your friends and relatives who have food allergies to share their experiences
* Identify and adapt your child's favorite recipes with alternative ingredients
* Explore chat rooms on the Internet - several sites exist for children with food allergies and their families

The goal is to set the proper tone for your child's future. He needs to feel comfortable with who he is in order to begin moving ahead. Establishing a matter-of-fact attitude about his diet is part of developing a positive self-image. This is an ongoing interactive process between you and your child. Continue to guide each other through this confusing time by remembering to keep the lines of communication open.

Can There be a Happy Ending?
Children who have food allergies will need some extra attention. Fortunately, there are a lot of resources available to you and places you can turn to for help. The most important thing to remember is that you are not alone. There is plenty of support out there if you reach for it. Keep an open mind and think positive. Your child will take his cues from you. It won't be easy, but you will get through this!

Don't Forget

Recognize the signs and symptoms of food allergies

Consult your pediatrician and/or pediatric allergist

Ask questions

Listen and talk to your child

Familiarize yourself with food labels and learn to recognize hidden ingredients

Plan ahead

Adapt favorite recipes

★ Communicate with: siblings, grandparents, babysitters, teachers ...everyone

Be supportive of your child's emotional well being

Create your own support system by making use of available resources

Remember Emily? After the panic subsided, Emily's parents did some research and found new recipes for her favorite foods. It took a great deal of hunting and an enormous amount of experimenting. Even though they don't taste exactly the same, Emily still gets to eat her favorite food - pancakes!

Chapter 2

How do I help my child meet her nutritional needs?

Did you know that less than 20 percent of all children eat the recommended servings of fruit and vegetables daily?

Proper nutrition is a significant part of our lives. That's why educating the entire family about healthy eating habits is essential. The United States Department of Agriculture (USDA), in conjunction with the Department of Health and Human Services, has developed guidelines for teaching people how to eat healthy. The Dietary Guidelines for Americans (age 2 years and older) provides the most current nutritional information available. Your whole family will benefit from following these guidelines. It is important that parents understand the nutritional needs of their child. Even though she requires a special diet, the basic principles of good nutrition should still be maintained.

The Dietary Guidelines for Americans

★ *Eat a variety of foods* to get the energy, protein, vitamins, minerals and fiber you need for good health.

★ *Balance the food you eat with physical activity;* maintain or improve your weight to reduce your chances of having high blood pressure, heart disease, a stroke, certain cancers and the most common kind of diabetes.

★ *Choose a diet with plenty of grain products, vegetables and fruits,* which provide needed vitamins, minerals, fiber and complex carbohydrates and can help you lower your intake of fat.

★ *Choose a diet low in fat, saturated fat and cholesterol* to reduce your risk of heart attack and certain types of cancer and to help you maintain a healthy weight.

★ *Choose a diet moderate in sugars.* A diet with lots of sugars has too many calories and too few nutrients for most people and can contribute to tooth decay.

★ *Choose a diet moderate in salt and sodium* to help reduce your risk of high blood pressure.

★ *If you drink alcoholic beverages, do so in moderation.* Alcoholic beverages supply calories, but little or no nutrients. Drinking alcohol is also the cause of many health problems and accidents and can lead to addiction.

What foods should my child be eating?

Children, as well as adults, need to eat a variety of foods each day. The Food Guide Pyramid was designed to help you make the right choices about the types of food and portion sizes necessary to promote good health. It can be used as a tool to help you decide what is right for your child's diet. The base of the pyramid contains foods that should be the foundation of your diet. These are the foods you should be eating the most of every day. Foods closer to the top should be eaten less frequently, and foods at the tip of the pyramid should only be eaten sparingly. Use the Food Guide Pyramid to help plan your meals. By following the recommended number of servings for each food group, you will be taking a giant step toward meeting the USDA Dietary Guidelines.

Food Guide Pyramid

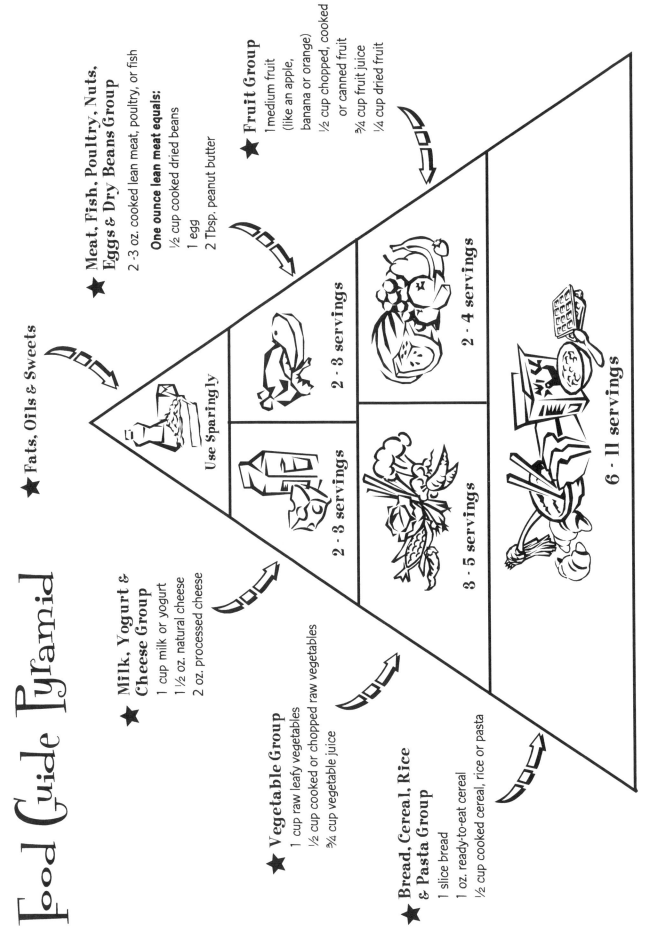

★ Fats, Oils & Sweets

★ **Meat, Fish, Poultry, Nuts, Eggs & Dry Beans Group**
2 - 3 oz. cooked lean meat, poultry, or fish

One ounce lean meat equals:
½ cup cooked dried beans
1 egg
2 Tbsp. peanut butter

★ **Fruit Group**
1 medium fruit
(like an apple,
banana or orange)
½ cup chopped, cooked
or canned fruit
¾ cup fruit juice
¼ cup dried fruit

★ **Milk, Yogurt & Cheese Group**
1 cup milk or yogurt
1 ½ oz. natural cheese
2 oz. processed cheese

★ **Vegetable Group**
1 cup raw leafy vegetables
½ cup cooked or chopped raw vegetables
¾ cup vegetable juice

★ **Bread, Cereal, Rice & Pasta Group**
1 slice bread
1 oz. ready-to-eat cereal
½ cup cooked cereal, rice or pasta

Use Sparingly

2 - 3 servings

2 - 4 servings

2 - 3 servings

3 - 5 servings

6 - 11 servings

Can the Food Pyramid be used for children on special diets?
Maintaining a balanced diet is important for everyone. The challenge is to use the Pyramid to help you meet your child's specific dietary requirements. If your child is allergic to gluten, using soy flour in a recipe might be a good option. Find an alternative source of calcium (such as tofu) if your child cannot have dairy products. Learning about appropriate substitutions for foods that must be omitted from your child's diet is the key. For a list of food substitutions see Chapter 3.

Remember to keep your child involved in making these choices. Meals should be planned together, allowing your child to make appropriate food choices within the Pyramid's guidelines. Your child's pediatrician, teacher, school nurse, school food service provider, nutritionist or allergist can be extremely helpful in this process. Early education will help to establish healthy eating habits throughout your child's life.

How much should my child be eating?
The total amount of calories your child needs each day depends upon a variety of factors. While the National Academy of Sciences recommends that the average child consume 2,200 calories per day, a preschool child may need to consume less than 1,600. Your pediatrician can help you plan what's right for your child's diet. Use this chart as a guide to help determine your child's daily caloric intake.

Age	Calorie Needs (kcal)
1-3 years	900-1800
4 -6 years	1300-2300
7-10 years	1650-3300

Developing an understanding about nutrition can be fun. Our **Daily Food Chart** will help your child visualize how she can meet her daily requirements. You should look at this chart together. A few minutes spent together each day demonstrate your commitment to helping your child take control of her own diet. It also shows your ongoing support.

Daily Food Chart

(Child's Name)

	Grains	Vegetables	Fruits	Meat	Milk
Serving 1					
Serving 2					
Serving 3					
Serving 4					
Serving 5					
Serving 6					
Serving 7					
Serving 8					
Serving 9					
Serving 10					
Serving 11					

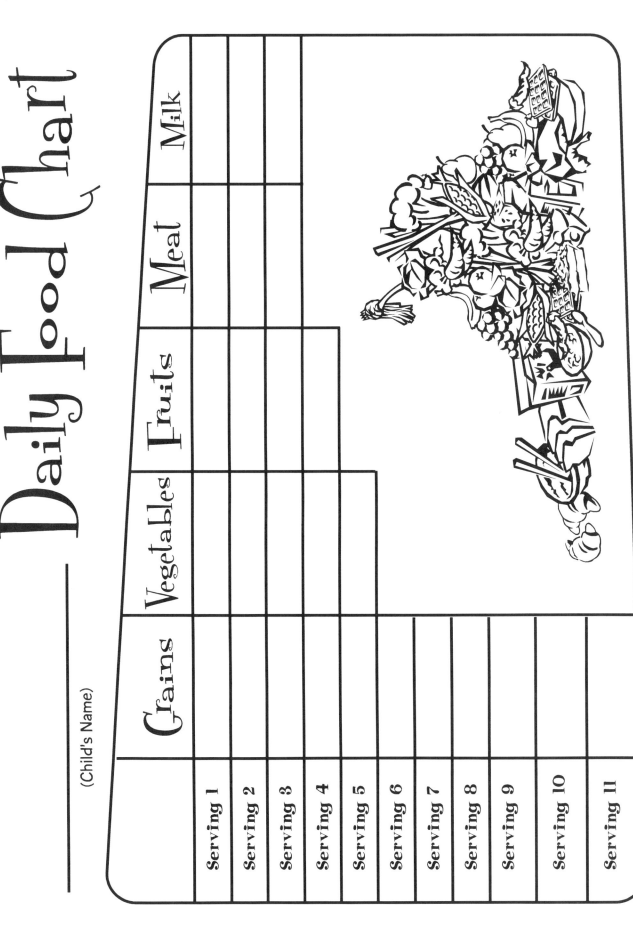

How do I know what foods are safe for my child?

Foods are grouped into categories, or food families. If you are allergic to a particular food it is possible you may also have a reaction to other members of that same food group. For example, if your child is allergic to cow's milk she may also be allergic to goat's milk. A gluten allergy (the grass/cereal family) may also mean an allergy to bamboo or sugar cane. Consultation with your pediatrician or allergist, along with careful controlled experimentation, will help you to discover exactly which foods your child should avoid.

Learn to read food labels! This is extremely important since so many of your child's favorite foods may contain hidden allergens. A tremendous amount of information is available if you look for it. All food products must now have a Nutrition Facts label, along with a complete list of ingredients. Familiarize yourself with these labels. Manufacturers often alter their recipes, so you must check the ingredients each and every time you shop.

Ask questions about food preparation. If you are unsure about an ingredient or have a question concerning how a food was made, call the company. Most labels will give you an address and/or telephone number for inquiries. The Food Allergy Network (see Resource List) is also an excellent source of information for answering your questions.

Begin familiarizing your family with all of the names for foods your child cannot tolerate. Use the Examples of Alternative Names for Food Allergens chart as a starting point.

Examples of Alternative Names for Food Allergens

DAIRY	EGGS	GLUTEN
casein	albumin	modified food starch
lactose	ovomucoid	alcohol extract
whey	ovalbumin	white vinegar
lactalbumin	ovomucin	wheat, rye, barley, oats, bran
lactoglobulin	livetein	vegetable gums
caseinate	ovotellin	malt
lactate	vitellin	hydrolyzed vegetable protein

Make a list of the foods your child should not be eating and carry copies as a reminder. This will make reading food labels easier and help with proper meal planning.

Good nutrition? I'm no health nut!

You don't have to be a nutrition expert, just an informed parent.

Remember

★ Everyone should follow the basic principles of good nutrition.

★ The USDA Dietary Guidelines teach people about healthy eating.

★ The Food Guide Pyramid provides a blueprint for meal planning.

★ Determine your child's daily calorie needs.

★ Use our Daily Food Chart to help your child take responsibility for making healthy food choices.

★ Determine what foods are safe for your child to eat.

★ Carefully read all food labels and check for hidden ingredients that might trigger an allergic reaction.

Understand that your influence as a parent will help shape your child's attitude towards food. A food allergy should not exclude your child from being able to maintain a healthy, balanced diet. You can lead the way.

Chapter 3

Help is on the way!

What foods can my child with food allergies eat?

Research demonstrates that avoidance is the best treatment for food allergies and intolerance. Ninety five percent of allergies in children are due to milk, eggs, wheat, soybeans, seafood, nuts and peanuts (which are legumes). If your child is allergic to any of these foods, you will probably spend considerable time searching for comparable food alternatives or substitutions. This cookbook contains recipes that offer substitutes for the ingredients that constitute several of the most common childhood food allergies: dairy products, gluten and eggs.

What about dairy products?

People with milk allergies are unable to digest the protein found in cow's milk. Ingesting even small amounts can trigger severe reactions that could range from runny noses and rashes to vomiting and breathing difficulties.[i] The Food Allergy Network estimates that 7.5 percent of children suffer from a milk allergy at some point in their lives.[ii]

Lactose intolerance is a condition where the body lacks the enzyme "lactase". Undigested, lactose passes into the intestinal tract where it can produce abdominal pain, diarrhea, bloating and gas. Approximately 4 percent of the population have lactose intolerance. This increases to as high as 90 percent among African Americans, Native Americans, Asians and people of Mediterranean descent.[iii]

A helpful tool when food shopping, is to look for the word "pareve" on product labels. This term is used to delineate kosher products that are dairy-free.

```
┌─────────────────────────────────────────────────────────────┐
│  COMMON SUBSTITUTES FOR MILK AND MILK PRODUCTS                │
│  Use equal amounts for substitution (example: 1 cup rice milk = 1 cup milk)  │
```

MILK	BUTTER	CHEESE	ICE CREAM
water	non-dairy margarine**	goat cheese*	sorbet
fruit juice	goat's milk butter*	tofu	milk-free sherbet
goat's milk*	soft tofu	nut cheese products	tofu ice cream
nut milk	vegetable oil	soy cheese products	rice milk ice cream
rice milk	fruit puree		
non-dairy** creamer	non-dairy shortening**		
soy milk			

★ If you are allergic to the casein in cow's milk, you may also be allergic to the casein in goat's milk.

★★ Some non-dairy creamers may contain "hidden" forms of dairy. Pay careful attention to the ingredient labels.

What do I do about a gluten allergy?

Celiac sprue is a condition in which the substance "gluten" can not be digested properly. Gluten can be found in grains, specifically wheat, rye, barley and sometimes oats. It can also be found in some grain products such as all-purpose flour, alcohol, flavored extracts and malt. Celiac disease occurs in about one of 2,000 to 3,000 Caucasians in North America.[iv] However, European studies have shown that the prevalence of childhood celiac disease is on the rise and predict a large increase by the year 2000.[v]

Gluten-free baking can be tricky. It may require a lower oven temperature and longer baking time. The taste, texture and color of alternative flours vary. In developing the recipes in this book, we found that rice flour works best as the basic substitute. We also found that rice flour can be very "grainy." A combination of several flours will go a long way to help alleviate this problem. Remember that alcohol contains gluten. Be sure to use pure flavorings, not extracts. The object is to arrive at a finished product that closely resembles the original.

The gluten found in flour is what holds baked goods together when they rise. Without it, bread tends to be heavier and denser; cookies tend to crumble easily. To overcome this problem something must be added. The recommended ingredient to add is xanthan gum (which can be found in most health food stores). A general formula is to add 1 teaspoon of xanthan gum for each cup of flour in your recipe.

SUBSTITUTIONS FOR ALL–PURPOSE FLOUR
1 cup all-purpose flour equals:

⅞ cup rice flour (brown or white)	1 cup corn meal
¾ cup soy flour	1 cup tapioca flour
⅝ cup potato starch flour	¾ cup chick pea flour
¾ cup potato starch	⅞ cup garbanzo bean flour
1 cup corn flour	

What about eggs?

Ovalbumin, a protein found in the whites of eggs, is the most frequent cause of allergic reactions. Eggs are frequently found in many processed foods. Egg whites are used to give baked goods a glazed effect. Even "egg substitutes" may have egg whites as an ingredient. Egg allergies have been reported in 4 percent of all infants. The probability increases to 8 percent in children who have been identified as being at-risk for allergic tendencies, because their parents have allergies.[vi]

COMMON SUBSTITUTIONS FOR EGGS

AS A BINDER	AS A THICKENER	AS A LEAVENING AGENT	AS A GLAZE
COMMERCIAL EGG REPLACER	COMMERCIAL EGG REPLACER	COMMERCIAL EGG REPLACER	MILK
ARROWROOT POWDER [use 1 Tbsp. for every cup of non-glutenous flour]	APPLESAUCE [¼ cup = 1 egg]	BAKING POWDER [1 tsp. = 1 egg]	BUTTER OR MARGARINE
GELATIN [Dissolve 1 tsp. in 3 Tbsp. boiling water. Freeze until thickened. Beat until frothy]	TAPIOCA FLOUR [use 1 Tbsp. for every cup of non-glutenous flour]	VINEGAR [1 tsp. = 1 egg]	FRUIT JUICE OR PUREE
BANANA [½ banana = 1 egg]	BANANA [½ banana = 1 egg]		WATER
TOFU [¼ cup = 1 egg]	TOFU [¼ cup = 1 egg]		
FLAX SEED [boil ⅓ cup with 1 cup water for 15 minutes]	FRUIT PUREE [¼ cup = 1 egg]		

How will I manage to prepare meals for my child with all of these special substitutions?

Cooking for your child is not as hard as you imagine. You already know what your child can and cannot eat, hidden ingredients to look for in foods, how to talk with your child about his allergies and some basic substitutions for offending ingredients. All you need are some kid-friendly recipes to help put all the pieces of the puzzle together.

The recipes that appear in the recipe section of this book offer the combinations of ingredients that worked best after a great deal of experimentation. All have been taste tested by children with and without specific food allergies. While this book is not intended to be used as a special diet, the recipes have been created to assist families with children who face dairy, gluten and egg allergies by omitting these specific food offenders.

How do I find the recipes I need?

The recipe section of this book is organized by meal categories (breakfast, lunch, dinner, desserts, beverages, snacks). Each category has its own table of contents. This will help you to easily locate all of the recipes for a particular meal. The recipes include serving suggestions, a nutritional analysis and recipe variations. Each dish features a base recipe, followed by preparation alternatives for all of the dietary restrictions addressed. Many of these recipes can be served to children who have multiple food allergies. Each one has been tested and is guaranteed to produce a finished product that will satisfy a child's taste buds as well as help alleviate his or her allergic condition.

How will I know which food substitutions to use?

The recipes are written to help you easily find the correct substitutions for your child's diet. Look for the identifying symbol and follow the recipe making the appropriate substitutions.

DAIRY ALLERGY

GLUTEN ALLERGY

EGG ALLERGY

Now it's time to start cooking. Pick a recipe and have fun!

Recipes

Breakfast recipes

Apple Muffins
Banana Muffins
Biscuits
Blueberry Muffins
Corn Muffins
Pancake Paintings
Sticky Cinnamon Buns
Tortilla French Toast
Waffles

Apple Muffins

Yields 12 muffins

INGREDIENTS:

1 cup peeled, cored & diced apples
½ Tbsp. lemon juice
¼ cup granulated sugar
2 Tbsp. brown sugar
½ cup unsweetened applesauce

¼ cup melted margarine
3 egg whites
1¾ cups all-purpose flour
2½ tsp. baking powder
½ tsp. salt
¾ tsp. cinnamon

PREHEAT oven to 400° F.
GREASE muffin tins or line with bake cups.
TOSS diced apples with lemon juice & set aside.
MIX sugar, brown sugar & applesauce together.
ADD melted margarine & egg whites, stir to mix.
COMBINE in a separate bowl; flour, baking powder, salt & cinnamon.
ADD dry ingredients to sugar mixture & mix to form batter.
ADD apples & gently stir into batter.
SPOON batter into prepared tins, approximately ⅔ full.
BAKE 18 - 20 minutes or until golden brown.
SERVE.

Use milk-free margarine.

Substitute ¾ cup plus 2 Tbsp. sweet rice flour mixed with ¾ cup corn starch for all-purpose flour.

Substitute ¼ cup water mixed with 3 tsp. powdered egg replacer for egg whites.

Nutritional Analysis:
(for base recipe)
Serving Size = 1 muffin

Calories (kcal):	139.2
Total Fat (g):	4.0
Saturated Fat (g):	0.8
Cholesterol (mg):	0
Carbohydrate (g):	23.3
Protein (g):	2.8
Sodium (mg):	258.0
Dietary Fiber (g):	0.9

Banana Muffins

Yields 18 muffins

INGREDIENTS:

⅓ cup sugar

1 cup unsweetened applesauce

3 very ripe bananas, frozen & defrosted

3 egg whites

1¾ cups all-purpose flour

2½ tsp. baking powder

½ tsp. salt

PREHEAT oven to 400° F.

GREASE muffin tins or line with bake cups.

MIX sugar & applesauce together.

MASH bananas into mixture.

ADD egg whites.

COMBINE flour, baking powder & salt in separate bowl.

ADD dry ingredients to banana mixture to form batter.

SPOON batter into prepared tins, approximately ⅔ full.

BAKE 18 - 20 minutes or until golden brown.

SERVE.

 Variations: Add ¾ cup chopped nuts, chocolate chips or raisins to batter.

No substitutions needed.

Substitute ¾ cup plus 2 Tbsp. brown rice flour mixed with ¾ cup corn starch.

Substitute ¼ cup water mixed with 3 tsp. powdered egg replacement for egg whites.

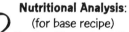

Nutritional Analysis:
(for base recipe)
Serving Size = 1 muffin

Calories (kcal):	84.6
Total Fat (g):	0.2
Saturated Fat (g):	0.1
Cholesterol (mg):	0
Carbohydrate (g):	19.1
Protein (g):	2.0
Sodium (mg):	142.1
Dietary Fiber (g):	1.0

Biscuits

Yields 24 biscuits

INGREDIENTS:

Flax + hemp Seed

1¾ cups all-purpose flour
½ tsp. salt
2 tsp. baking powder
1 tsp. baking soda

3 Tbsp. chilled margarine
2 Tbsp. vegetable shortening
⅔ cup water
1 Tbsp. melted margarine

PREHEAT oven to 450° F.

SIFT together flour, salt, baking powder, & baking soda.

CUT in chilled margarine & shortening using a pastry blender or two knives until consistency of small beads.

FORM well in center of mixture.

POUR water into well & mix to form dough.

TURN dough onto lightly floured board & kneed for approximately 30 seconds.

ROLL out dough using a floured rolling pin to ¼ inch thickness.

CUT into 2 inch rounds.

PLACE on <u>ungreased</u> cookie sheet.

BRUSH top of biscuits with melted margarine.

BAKE for 10 minutes or until golden brown.

SERVE.

 Use milk-free margarine.

 Substitute 1 cup rice flour & ¾ cup potato starch flour for all-purpose flour. Increase baking powder to 4 tsp. Add 1 tsp. xanthan gum. Substitute ½ cup club soda plus 1 beaten egg for water. Substitute egg wash★ for melted margarine.

 No substitutions needed.

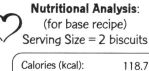

Nutritional Analysis:
(for base recipe)
Serving Size = 2 biscuits

Calories (kcal):	118.7
Total Fat (g):	6.1
Saturated Fat (g):	1.3
Cholesterol (mg):	0
Carbohydrate (g):	14.0
Protein (g):	1.9
Sodium (mg):	283.9
Dietary Fiber (g):	.5

★ To make egg wash: beat one egg with a small amount of milk or water.

Blueberry Muffins

Yields 12 muffins

INGREDIENTS:

¼ cup sugar
¼ cup unsweetened applesauce
1 tsp. vanilla
¼ cup melted margarine
3 egg whites

1¾ cups all-purpose flour
2½ tsp. baking powder
½ tsp. salt
1 cup blueberries (fresh or frozen)

PREHEAT oven to 400° F.
GREASE muffin tins or line with bake cups.
MIX sugar, applesauce & vanilla together.
ADD melted margarine & egg whites, stir to mix.
COMBINE flour, baking powder & salt in a separate bowl.
ADD dry ingredients to sugar mixture & mix to form batter.
FOLD blueberries into batter.
SPOON batter into prepared tins, approximately ⅔ full.
BAKE 18 minutes or until golden brown.
SERVE.

Use milk-free margarine.

Substitute ¾ cup plus 2 Tbsp. sweet rice flour
mixed with ¾ cup corn starch for all-purpose flour.

Substitute ¼ cup water mixed with 3 tsp.
powdered egg replacer for egg whites.

Nutritional Analysis:
(for base recipe)
Serving Size = 1 muffin

Calories (kcal):	135.9
Total Fat (g):	4.0
Saturated Fat (g):	0.8
Cholesterol (mg):	0
Carbohydrate (g):	22.1
Protein (g):	2.9
Sodium (mg):	257.6
Dietary Fiber (g):	0.9

Corn Muffins

Yields 12 muffins

INGREDIENTS:

1½ cups yellow cornmeal
½ cup all-purpose flour
3 tsp. baking powder
¼ cup sugar
1 tsp. dried orange peel
½ tsp. salt
1 egg
1 cup milk
4 Tbsp. margarine, melted
½ cup unsweetened applesauce

PREHEAT oven to 400° F.
MIX dry ingredients in bowl.
ADD remaining ingredients.
MIX by hand until batter forms.
SPOON into well greased muffin tins.
BAKE 12-15 minutes .
SERVE warm.

 Recipe Variation: Bake in loaf pan for 30 - 35 minutes, until toothpick comes out clean.

Use equal amounts of milk substitute & milk-free margarine.

Substitute ½ cup corn flour for all-purpose flour.

Omit egg & increase applesauce to ¾ cup.

Nutritional Analysis:
(for base recipe)
Serving Size = 1 muffin

Calories (kcal):	152.4
Total Fat (g):	5.4
Saturated Fat (g):	1.4
Cholesterol (mg):	20.6
Carbohydrate (g):	23.3
Protein (g):	3.1
Sodium (mg):	281.7
Dietary Fiber (g):	1.6

Pancake Paintings

Yields 8 pancakes

INGREDIENTS:

1 cup all-purpose flour
1 tsp. baking powder
1 cup milk
1 Tbsp. safflower oil
2 tsp. vanilla
1 egg
2 Tbsp. club soda

MIX flour & baking powder together in a bowl.
ADD milk gradually & stir to mix.
ADD oil, vanilla, & egg & beat or whisk until smooth.
ADD club soda & whisk for 1 minute.
POUR 2 Tbsp. batter onto very hot non-stick griddle or frying pan (use shortening to grease pan if needed).
COOK until pancakes have a bubbly surface & slightly dry edges.
FLIP & continue cooking until golden brown.
SERVE immediately with "Pancake Paint" (see recipe).

Substitute ½ cup apple juice & ½ cup water for milk.

Substitute 1 cup rice flour for all-purpose flour & add 1 tsp. sugar. Stir frequently as batter may separate.

Omit egg; increase baking powder to 2 tsp. & decrease milk to ¾ cup.

Nutritional Analysis:
(for base recipe)
Serving Size = 2 pancakes

Calories (kcal):	236
Total Fat (g):	10.4
Saturated Fat (g):	2.3
Cholesterol (mg):	61.4
Carbohydrate (g):	27.2
Protein (g):	6.7
Sodium (mg):	168.3
Dietary Fiber (g):	0.8

Sticky Cinnamon Buns

Yields 12 buns

INGREDIENTS:

¼ cup maple syrup
3 Tbsp. light brown sugar, packed
1½ tsp. margarine
½ Tbsp. water

"Biscuit Dough" (see recipe)
3 Tbsp. granulated sugar
½ tsp. ground cinnamon

PREHEAT oven to 425° F.

COMBINE maple syrup, brown sugar, margarine & water in saucepan.

COOK over low heat until brown sugar dissolves, stirring constantly (do <u>not</u> boil).

SPREAD mixture on bottom of 9 inch round pan.

ROLL OUT "Biscuit Dough" into a rectangle ¼ inch thick.

MIX together cinnamon & sugar in a separate bowl.

SPRINKLE cinnamon mixture evenly over dough.

ROLL UP jelly roll style, beginning with long side.

MOISTEN edge with water & crimp to seal.

SLICE dough into 1 inch thick pieces.

PLACE, sides down, in prepared pan.

BAKE for 20 minutes.

INVERT onto serving plate.

SERVE.

Recipe Variation: Sprinkle ⅓ cup coarsely chopped nuts over sugar mixture, in pan, before adding biscuits.

Use milk-free margarine.

Use gluten-free "Biscuit Dough" recipe.

No substitutions needed.

Nutritional Analysis:
(for base recipe)
Serving Size = 1 bun

Calories (kcal):	174.2
Total Fat (g):	7.5
Saturated Fat (g):	1.5
Cholesterol (mg):	0
Carbohydrate (g):	25.1
Protein (g):	1.9
Sodium (mg):	302.6
Dietary Fiber (g):	0.5

Tortilla French Toast

Yields 12 tortilla "toasts"

INGREDIENTS:

12 "Tortillas" (see recipe)
4 apples, peeled, cored & diced
¼ cup orange juice
1¾ tsp. cinnamon
1 Tbsp. brown sugar
2 tsp. vanilla

1 Tbsp. margarine
¼ cup apricot preserves
1 cup raisins
2 eggs
1 Tbsp. milk
margarine for frying

TOSS apples with orange juice to coat.
ADD 1 ½ tsp. cinnamon, brown sugar & 1 ½ tsp. vanilla.
MELT 1 Tbsp. margarine in a pan.
ADD apple mixture.
SAUTE until slightly soft & remove from heat.
ADD apricot preserves & raisins.
STIR to mix.
SET ASIDE.
COMBINE eggs, milk, ¼ tsp. cinnamon & ½ tsp. vanilla.
SOAK each tortilla in egg mixture.
PRICK tortilla using tines of fork.
FRY tortilla on greased griddle until both sides are browned & puffed slightly.
REMOVE from pan.
PLACE 1 heaping Tbsp. of fruit mixture in center of tortilla.
ROLL & place on serving plate, seam side down.
REPEAT using remaining tortillas.
SPOON remaining fruit mixture over tortillas.
SERVE immediately.

Substitute 1 Tbsp. apple juice for milk.
Use milk-free margarine.

No substitutions needed.

Substitute ½ cup apple juice at room temperature &
¼ cup melted margarine for eggs & milk.

Nutritional Analysis:
(for base recipe)
Serving Size = 2 tortillas

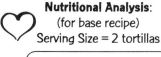

Calories (kcal):	491.8
Total Fat (g):	7.0
Saturated Fat (g):	1.4
Cholesterol (mg):	71.2
Carbohydrate (g):	102.4
Protein (g):	10.4
Sodium (mg):	253.3
Dietary Fiber (g):	10.4

Waffles

Yields 8 waffles

INGREDIENTS:

1 cup all-purpose flour
1 tsp. baking powder
1 tsp. sugar
1 cup milk
1 egg
1 Tbsp. vegetable oil
2 tsp. vanilla
2 Tbsp. club soda

HEAT waffle iron.
MIX flour, baking powder & sugar in bowl.
ADD milk gradually & stir to mix.
ADD egg, oil & vanilla.
BEAT or whisk until smooth.
ADD club soda.
WHISK for 1 minute.
POUR ½ cup batter into waffle iron.
COOK according to manufacturers directions.
SERVE immediately with syrup, preserves, etc.

 Serving suggestion: Make waffles ahead of time & store up to 2 weeks in freezer. Reheat in toaster.

 Substitute ½ cup apple juice & ½ cup water for milk.

Substitute 1 cup rice flour for all-purpose flour. Stir frequently as batter may separate.

Omit egg; increase baking powder to 2 tsp. & decrease milk to ¾ cup.

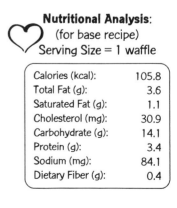

Nutritional Analysis:
(for base recipe)
Serving Size = 1 waffle

Calories (kcal):	105.8
Total Fat (g):	3.6
Saturated Fat (g):	1.1
Cholesterol (mg):	30.9
Carbohydrate (g):	14.1
Protein (g):	3.4
Sodium (mg):	84.1
Dietary Fiber (g):	0.4

Lunch

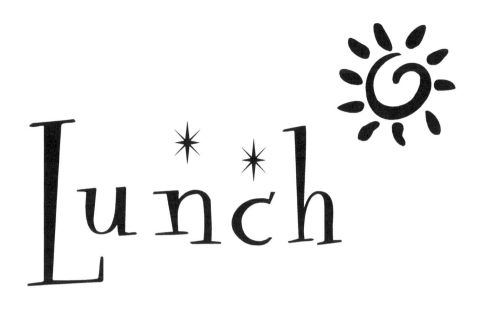

Bread Machine White Bread
Burger Dogs
Chicken Pinwheels
Chuck Wagon Bagoo
Corn Dogs
Meat Tostadas
Sombreros
Tortillas
Vegetable Fun-do

Bread Machine White Bread

Yields 1 loaf

INGREDIENTS:

2 ½ tsp. yeast
2 ⅓ cups all-purpose flour
1 ½ Tbsp. sugar
1 tsp. salt

1 Tbsp. vegetable oil
1 tsp. rice vinegar
1 egg
1 cup plus 1 Tbsp. hot water (110°F - 115°F)

PLACE yeast in bottom of bread machine.
COMBINE flour, sugar & salt in a bowl.
ADD to machine.
COMBINE oil, vinegar, egg & water.
ADD to machine.
SET controls to medium setting.
BAKE according to manufacturers directions.
SERVE.

No substitutions needed.

Increase yeast to 1 Tbsp. Substitute 1 cup corn flour, 1 cup rice flour & ⅓ cup potato starch for all-purpose flour. Add 2 tsp. xanthan gum.

Omit egg. Increase yeast to 1 Tbsp. Set controls to dark setting.

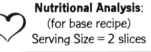

Nutritional Analysis:
(for base recipe)
Serving Size = 2 slices

Calories (kcal):	168.8
Total Fat (g):	2.7
Saturated Fat (g):	.5
Cholesterol (mg):	26.6
Carbohydrate (g):	30.5
Protein (g):	5.0
Sodium (mg):	300.9
Dietary Fiber (g):	1.2

Burger Dogs

Yields 6 "dogs"

INGREDIENTS:

1 lb. ground beef
1 tsp. garlic powder
1 tsp. onion powder
½ tsp. oregano
2 Tbsp. tomato paste
salt & pepper to taste

COMBINE all ingredients in bowl.
DIVIDE meat mixture into six equal portions.
ROLL each portion into six inch log.
BROIL, turning once, 8 - 12 minutes, or as long as desired.
SERVE on hot dog bun with your favorite burger toppings.

 No substitutions needed.

 No substitutions needed. Use gluten-free bun.

 No substitutions needed.

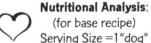

Nutritional Analysis:
(for base recipe)
Serving Size =1"dog"

Calories (kcal):	206.8
Total Fat (g):	15.7
Saturated Fat (g):	6.3
Cholesterol (mg):	56.7
Carbohydrate (g):	1.6
Protein (g):	13.7
Sodium (mg):	81.8
Dietary Fiber (g):	0.4

Chicken Pin Wheels

Yields 16 "pinwheels"

Finely chopped onion + spinach garlic
½ c. squash pureed

INGREDIENTS:

"Biscuit Dough" (see recipe)
3 cups cooked ground chicken
¼ tsp. garlic powder
¼ tsp. onion powder

salt & pepper to taste
2 Tbsp. melted margarine
1 Tbsp. chopped parsley or parsley flakes
⅛ tsp. paprika

PREHEAT oven to 450° F.

SEASON ground chicken with garlic powder, onion powder, salt & pepper & set aside. *Flavor Chix*

DIVIDE dough into 2 equal parts.

ROLL out one portion of dough to form a rectangle, ⅛ inch thick.

BRUSH with ½ Tbsp. melted margarine.

SPRINKLE dough with ½ Tbsp. parsley.

SPREAD with ½ of meat mixture to within one inch of edges.

ROLL to form log.

MOISTEN the end with water & pinch lightly to seal.

SPRINKLE with paprika.

CUT 1 inch thick slices & place on greased cookie sheet.

BRUSH with ½ Tbsp. melted margarine.

REPEAT with remaining ingredients.

BAKE for 15 minutes.

SERVE

Use milk-free margarine.

Use gluten-free "Biscuit Dough" (see recipe). Use 2 cups of meat mixture. Roll filled log carefully, repairing tears as they occur.

No substitutions needed.

Nutritional Analysis:
(for base recipe)
Serving Size = 1 "pin wheel"

Calories (kcal):	164.3
Total Fat (g):	9.1
Saturated Fat (g):	2.0
Cholesterol (mg):	21.8
Carbohydrate (g):	10.6
Protein (g):	9.4
Sodium (mg):	243.4
Dietary Fiber (g):	0.4

Chuck Wagon Bagoo

Yields 2 quarts

INGREDIENTS:

1 Tbsp. vegetable oil
⅓ cup diced onion
⅓ cup finely diced celery
2 cloves garlic, minced
1 lb. ground meat
2 Tbsp. brown sugar
28 oz. can whole peeled tomatoes
    in thick puree
½ lb. elbow pasta, cooked
15 oz. can red pinto beans,
    cooked & drained
salt & pepper to taste

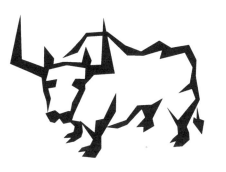

HEAT oil in skillet.
SAUTE onion, celery & garlic until soft.
SET ASIDE.
BROWN meat & drain off excess fat.
STIR in onion & celery mixture.
ADD brown sugar & tomatoes.
SIMMER to boil.
STIR in pasta & beans.
ADD salt & pepper to taste.
SIMMER until heated through.
SERVE.

No substitutions needed.

Use gluten-free pasta.

No substitutions needed.

Nutritional Analysis:
(for base recipe)
Serving Size = 1 cup

Calories (kcal):	288.0
Total Fat (g):	14.1
Saturated Fat (g):	5.1
Cholesterol (mg):	42.5
Carbohydrate (g):	24.7
Protein (g):	15.7
Sodium (mg):	445.5
Dietary Fiber (g):	3.4

Corn Dogs

Yields 8 corn dogs

INGREDIENTS:

4 hot dogs
1 cup yellow corn meal
2 Tbsp. all-purpose flour
½ tsp. baking power

½ tsp. salt
¼ cup milk
1 egg
oil for frying

CUT each hot dog in half.
COOK in boiling water for 5 minutes & set aside.
COMBINE corn meal, flour, baking powder & salt in a bowl.
BEAT milk & egg together in separate bowl.
ADD egg mixture to dry ingredients.
MIX to form dough.
FLATTEN 1 heaping Tbsp. of dough between slightly wet hands to form "pancake".
WRAP hot dog pieces in dough, covering completely.
REPEAT with remaining dough.
DEEP FRY until golden brown.
DRAIN on paper towels.
SERVE.

Substitute an equal amount of rice milk for milk.

Substitute 2 Tbsp. potato flour for all-purpose flour.

Substitute 1 ½ tsp. egg replacer mixed with 2 Tbsp. water for egg. Add an additional 2 Tbsp. milk.

Nutritional Analysis:
(for base recipe)
Serving Size = 2 corn dogs

Calories (kcal):	263.7
Total Fat (g):	9.2
Saturated Fat (g):	3.8
Cholesterol (mg):	79.1
Carbohydrate (g):	31.9
Protein (g):	12.6
Sodium (mg):	945.2
Dietary Fiber (g):	2.8

Meat Tostadas

Yields 12 tostadas

INGREDIENTS:

12 "tortillas" (see recipe)
1 lb. ground beef
½ tsp. onion powder
½ tsp. garlic powder
½ tsp. cumin
½ tsp. paprika
salt to taste
3 oz. cheddar cheese, shredded
1 cup shredded lettuce
½ cup diced tomatoes
oil for frying

HEAT oil in large skillet (approx. ½ inch).
FRY tortillas in oil, one at a time until slightly brown (approx. 30 seconds per side).
DRAIN on paper towels & set aside.
BROWN meat with onion powder, garlic powder, cumin, paprika & salt.
DRAIN excess fat.
PLACE each tortilla on plate & layer meat, lettuce, tomato & cheese.
SERVE with guacamole or salsa.

Recipe Variation: Use taco shell basket to deep fry tortillas to produce crispy taco shells. Fill with same ingredients & serve. For a meatless lunch, substitute tuna salad for meat.

Use milk-free cheddar cheese.

No substitutions needed.

No substitutions needed.

Nutritional Analysis:
(for base recipe)
Serving Size = 2 tostadas

Calories (kcal):	546.2
Total Fat (g):	24.1
Saturated Fat (g):	9.8
Cholesterol (mg):	71.6
Carbohydrate (g):	59.2
Protein (g):	24.3
Sodium (mg):	368.0
Dietary Fiber (g):	7.6

49

Sombreros

Yields 12 "sombreros"

FILLING:

1 lb. ground beef
2 Tbsp. minced onion
1 tsp. olive oil
1 medium carrot, shredded
1 tsp. minced garlic
¾ cup plus 1 Tbsp. tomato puree
¼ tsp. salt
1 tsp. chili powder
2 Tbsp. water

> **PREHEAT** oven to 400° F.
> **BROWN** ground beef in pan.
> **DRAIN** off fat & set aside.
> **SAUTE** onion & carrot in oil until soft.
> **ADD** garlic & cook for an additional minute.
> **ADD** ¾ cup tomato puree, salt & chili powder.
> **BRING** to a boil.
> **COMBINE** puree mixture with meat & set aside.

DOUGH:

2 ½ cups masa harina★
1 ¼ tsp. salt
⅓ cup plus 3 Tbsp. margarine
⅓ cup vegetable shortening
8 Tbsp. ice water

> **MIX** masa harina & salt.
> **CUT** in shortening & margarine using 2 knives or hands until consistency of peas.
> **ADD** water to form dough.
> **TURN** small portions of dough onto board, lightly floured with masa harina.
> **ROLL** to ⅛ inch thickness.
> **CUT** into 4 inch rounds.

TO FORM SOMBREROS:

> **PLACE** round on <u>ungreased</u> cookie sheet.
> **SCOOP** 2 Tbsp. of meat mixture onto center of round.
> **MOISTEN** edge with water.
> **TOP** with additional round & seal using tines of fork.
> **MIX** 1 Tbsp. tomato puree & water together to make "wash".
> **BRUSH** tomato wash over "sombreros".
> **BAKE** for 20 - 25 minutes or until golden brown.
> **TOP** with Sombrero Sauce.

 ★ masa harina: ground corn treated with lime water. Available in most grocery stores.

SOMBRERO SAUCE:

2 tsp. olive oil
2 Tbsp. minced onion
½ cup minced roasted peppers
1 tsp. chili powder
1 cup tomato puree

SAUTE onions in oil until soft.
ADD roasted peppers & garlic & cook until heated through.
MIX in chili powder & tomato puree.
BRING to boil.
REMOVE from heat.
TOP each "Sombrero" with ½ tsp. sauce.
SERVE.

Use milk-free margarine.

No substitutions needed.

No substitutions needed.

♡ **Nutritional Analysis**:
(for base recipe)
Serving Size = 1 "sombrero"

Calories (kcal):	440.1
Total Fat (g):	26.5
Saturated Fat (g):	7.4
Cholesterol (mg):	32.1
Carbohydrate (g):	41.1
Protein (g):	11.5
Sodium (mg):	355.7
Dietary Fiber (g):	5.7

Tortillas

INGREDIENTS:

2 cup masa harina*
1 ½ cups warm water
½ tsp. salt

Yields approx. 12 tortillas

MIX ingredients to form dough.
DIVIDE into 12 equal parts.
LET rest for 10 minutes.
PLACE One part dough between 2 pieces of wax paper.
ROLL out to form 6 inch round or use tortilla press.
REPEAT with remaining dough.
PREHEAT griddle or skillet over medium heat.
PEEL off top piece of wax paper & place tortilla in pan.
HEAT slightly, being careful not to allow paper to burn.
REMOVE second piece of wax paper & cook until dry around edge, about 1 minute.
FLIP tortilla & cook for additional 1 - 2 minutes.
STACK tortillas between pieces of wax paper until ready to use.
REFRIGERATE in airtight container, if not immediately used.

Cold tortillas can be reheated. Place in microwave & cover with damp paper towel. Heat on high for 10 seconds. If dry, sprinkle with water.

 Recipe Variation: Add your favorite seasonings to flour mixture (garlic, chili powder, etc.)

★ *masa harina: ground corn treated with lime water. Available in most grocery stores.*

 Nutritional Analysis:
Serving Size = 2 tortillas

Calories (kcal):	275.9
Total Fat (g):	2.8
Saturated Fat (g):	0.4
Cholesterol (mg):	0
Carbohydrate (g):	57.6
Protein (g):	7.1
Sodium (mg):	199.3
Dietary Fiber (g):	7.2

No substitutions needed.

Vegetable Fun-do

Yields approx. 40 vegetable balls.

INGREDIENTS:

1 Tbsp. olive oil
2 garlic cloves, minced
1 celery stalk, minced
¼ cup minced onion
2 cups mixed vegetables,* cooked
1 cup mashed potatoes

3 Tbsp. tomato paste
1 egg, beaten
6 Tbsp. white cornmeal
3 Tbsp. potato starch flour
salt & pepper to taste
oil for frying
"Cheese Sauce" (see recipe)

★ string beans, corn, carrots, peas etc.

SAUTE garlic, celery & onion in olive oil until soft.
COMBINE vegetables with sauteed mixture in food processor.
BLEND to form a thick paste.
COMBINE potatoes & tomato paste in separate bowl.
ADD egg, cornmeal & potato starch flour & stir to mix.
FOLD in vegetable paste.
ADD salt & pepper.
FORM into tablespoon size balls.
HEAT oil for deep frying (375°).
DEEP FRY until golden brown.
DRAIN on paper towels & keep warm in a 200°F. oven.
PREPARE "Cheese Sauce".
PLACE sauce in fondue pot or in top of double boiler.
SPEAR vegetable balls with toothpicks, skewers or forks & dunk into "Cheese Sauce".

Recipe Variation: Bake vegetable balls on oiled cookie sheet at 350° F. for 15 minutes. Turn over & continue baking for an additional 10 minutes.

No substitutions needed.

No substitutions needed.

Substitute 2 Tbsp. water mixed together with 1 ½ tsp. egg replacer for egg.

Nutritional Analysis:
(for base recipe)
Serving Size = 4 vegetable balls with 1½ oz. cheese sauce

Calories (kcal):	144.8
Total Fat (g):	4.5
Saturated Fat (g):	1.8
Cholesterol (mg):	31.4
Carbohydrate (g):	21.9
Protein (g):	5.2
Sodium (mg):	209.7
Dietary Fiber (g):	2.8

Soup

Chicken Stock
Fruit Soup
Pizza Soup
Potato Cheese Soup
Teriyaki Chicken Soup
with Rice AWARD WINNING RECIPE

Chicken Stock

Yields 2 quarts

INGREDIENTS:

1 chicken, skinned & cut into pieces
8 carrots, quartered
6 celery stalks, quartered
1 turnip, quartered
10 sprigs dill
2 parsnips, quartered
1 leek, halved
6 sprigs parsley
1 onion, quartered
3 quarts cold water

PLACE ingredients in pot.
BRING to boil.
REDUCE heat.
SIMMER for 1 ½ hours.
STRAIN soup.
SERVE.

 Recipe Variation: For a vegetable chicken soup, serve without straining.

No substitutions needed.

No substitutions needed.

No substitutions needed.

Nutritional Analysis:
(for base recipe)
Serving Size = 8 oz.

Calories (kcal):	150.3
Total Fat (g):	2.8
Saturated Fat (g):	0.7
Cholesterol (mg):	57.6
Carbohydrate (g):	12.3
Protein (g):	19.0
Sodium (mg):	134.2
Dietary Fiber (g):	3.4

Fruit Soup

Yields 2 quarts

INGREDIENTS:

1 lb. pitted cherries
2 medium pears, cored & diced
3 plums, pitted, peeled, & diced
2 peaches, pitted, peeled & diced
½ lemon, juice & pulp
½ lime, juice & pulp
1 cup orange juice
2 cups water
1 cup sugar
2 tsp. vanilla

PLACE ingredients in pot.
BRING to boil.
SIMMER until fruit is soft (approx. 1 hour), stirring occasionally.
PUREE until smooth.
CHILL.
SERVE.

 Serving Suggestion: Top with seasonal fruit (blueberries) & /or vanilla ice cream, whipped cream or yogurt.

No substitutions needed.

No substitutions needed.

No substitutions needed.

Nutritional Analysis:
(for base recipe)
Serving Size = 8oz.

Calories (kcal):	206.0
Total Fat (g):	1.0
Saturated Fat (g):	0.2
Cholesterol (mg):	0
Carbohydrate (g):	50.1
Protein (g):	1.5
Sodium (mg):	2.6
Dietary Fiber (g):	3.4

PiZZa Soup

Yields 5 cups

INGREDIENTS:

1 qt. strained tomatoes
1 ½ cups cold water
1 tsp. garlic powder
1 tsp. onion powder
½ tsp. oregano
½ tsp. basil
½ tsp. parsley flakes
1 Tbsp. sugar
1 ½ cups shredded
mozzarella cheese

MIX all ingredients (except cheese) in pot.
BRING to boil.
REDUCE heat & simmer for 15 minutes.
PORTION 8 oz. of soup into oven proof bowl.
SPRINKLE with ¼ cup cheese.
BROIL 2 - 3 minutes.
SERVE.

Substitute milk-free cheese.

No substitutions needed.

No substitutions needed.

 Nutritional Analysis:
(for base recipe)
Serving Size = 8oz.

Calories (kcal):	133.4
Total Fat (g):	5.6
Saturated Fat (g):	3.1
Cholesterol (mg):	15.4
Carbohydrate (g):	13.3
Protein (g):	9.6
Sodium (mg):	388.2
Dietary Fiber (g):	2.4

Potato Cheese Soup

Yields 4 cups

INGREDIENTS:

1 leek
2 Tbsp. margarine
5 medium potatoes, peeled &
    sliced thin
1 cup "Chicken Stock"(see recipe)

1 cup milk
¼ tsp. salt
⅛ tsp. white pepper
3 oz. cheddar cheese, shredded

SLICE the white part of the leek.
SAUTE in 1 Tbsp. margarine until soft.
ADD potatoes & enough water to cover.
BRING to boil & cook until soft (approx. 15 minutes).
DRAIN contents of pot & discard liquid.
ADD remaining Tbsp. margarine to potato & leek mixture.
PUREE until smooth.
RETURN to pot.
GRADUALLY ADD chicken stock & milk, stirring constantly.
HEAT over low flame.
ADD salt, pepper & cheese, stirring constantly until cheese melts
(be careful not to allow soup to come to full boil).
SERVE.

Use milk-free margarine & milk substitute (goat, soy, nut, etc.). Use milk-free cheese.

No substitutions needed.

No substitutions needed.

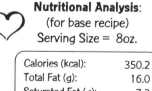

Nutritional Analysis:
(for base recipe)
Serving Size = 8oz.

Calories (kcal):	350.2
Total Fat (g):	16.0
Saturated Fat (g):	7.3
Cholesterol (mg):	48.3
Carbohydrate (g):	36.5
Protein (g):	16.4
Sodium (mg):	428.4
Dietary Fiber (g):	3.8

Teriyaki Chicken Soup with Rice

Yields 2 quarts

INGREDIENTS:

1 lb. boneless/skinless chicken breasts, sliced into strips
¼ cup teriyaki sauce
2 stalks celery
3 carrots
1 parsnip
3 scallions, bottom halves

1 clove garlic, whole
¼ tsp. ground ginger
¼ tsp. dry mustard
2 qts. "Chicken Stock" (see recipe)
1 Tbsp. oil
1 ½ cups cooked rice

MARINATE chicken in teriyaki sauce overnight.
CUT celery, carrots & parsnips into match stick slices & set aside.
SLICE scallions (thinly) & set aside.
HEAT chicken stock.
ADD chicken, garlic, ginger & mustard.
BRING to boil & simmer 15 minutes.
HEAT oil in sauce pan & saute vegetables until soft.

TO SERVE:
LADLE 6 oz. of soup into bowl.
ADD 2 ½ oz. of chicken, 2oz. of vegetables & ¼ cup rice.
SERVE.

AWARD WINNING RECIPE

No substitutions needed.

Use gluten-free teriyaki sauce.

No substitutions needed.

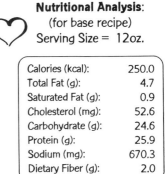

Nutritional Analysis:
(for base recipe)
Serving Size = 12oz.

Calories (kcal):	250.0
Total Fat (g):	4.7
Saturated Fat (g):	0.9
Cholesterol (mg):	52.6
Carbohydrate (g):	24.6
Protein (g):	25.9
Sodium (mg):	670.3
Dietary Fiber (g):	2.0

Salads

Apple Walnut Salad
Chicken & Grape Salad
Fruit Salad
Macaroni Salad
Pasta Salad
Potato Salad
Zucchini Slaw

Apple Walnut Salad

Yields 2 cups

INGREDIENTS:

2 cups cored & cubed apples
½ cup orange juice
¼ cup diced celery
2 Tbsp. chopped walnuts
2 Tbsp. raisins
3 - 4 Tbsp. plain yogurt
cinnamon to taste

POUR orange juice over apples & gently toss for 1 minute.
DRAIN & reserve 2 tsp. of orange juice.
COMBINE apples, orange juice & remaining ingredients in bowl.
TOSS to mix.
CHILL .
SERVE.

 Recipe Variation: Substitute 2 Tbsp. sliced almonds for walnuts.

Substitute ¼ cup silken tofu mixed with 4 tsp. orange juice for yogurt. Blend until smooth.

No substitutions needed.

No substitutions needed.

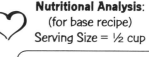

Nutritional Analysis:
(for base recipe)
Serving Size = ½ cup

Calories (kcal):	95.8
Total Fat (g):	3.0
Saturated Fat (g):	0.5
Cholesterol (mg):	2.0
Carbohydrate (g):	16.7
Protein (g):	2.0
Sodium (mg):	14.0
Dietary Fiber (g):	2.3

Chicken & Grape Salad

Yields 2 cups

INGREDIENTS:
2 cups cooked chicken, cubed
½ cup halved seedless red grapes
4 Tbsp. mayonnaise
2 heaping Tbsp. sliced almonds
white pepper & salt to taste

COMBINE ingredients in bowl.
SERVE.

 Serving Suggestion: Serve in scooped out tomatoes, cucumbers or zucchini.

 No substitutions needed.

Use "Eggless Mayonnaise II" (see recipe).

Use "Eggless Mayonnaise II" (see recipe).

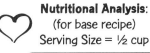 **Nutritional Analysis**:
(for base recipe)
Serving Size = ½ cup

Calories (kcal):	224.6
Total Fat (g):	12.8
Saturated Fat (g):	2.7
Cholesterol (mg):	60.0
Carbohydrate (g):	4.7
Protein (g):	22.1
Sodium (mg):	107.5
Dietary Fiber (g):	0.6

63

Fruit Salad

Yields 2 cups

INGREDIENTS:
2 cups cut-up fruit, in season
2 Tbsp. "Fruit Dressing" (see recipe)

COMBINE ingredients in bowl.
SERVE.

 Serving Suggestion: Sprinkle with chopped nuts or cinnamon.

No substitutions needed.

No substitutions needed.

No substitutions needed.

Nutritional Analysis:
(for base recipe)
Serving Size = ½ cup

Calories (kcal):	67.9
Total Fat (g):	0.3
Saturated Fat (g):	0.2
Cholesterol (mg):	1.0
Carbohydrate (g):	16.7
Protein (g):	0.9
Sodium (mg):	9.5
Dietary Fiber (g):	1.3

Macaroni Salad

Yields 2 cups

INGREDIENTS:
2 cups elbow pasta, cooked
2 Tbsp. finely diced carrot
2 Tbsp. diced celery
2 Tbsp. diced red bell pepper
½ tsp. onion powder
¼ tsp. garlic powder
4 Tbsp. mayonnaise
salt to taste

COMBINE ingredients in bowl.
TOSS to mix.
SERVE.

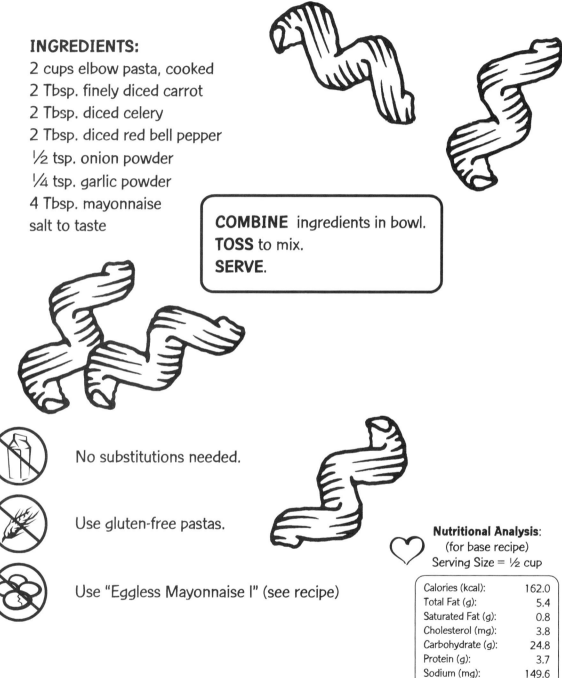

No substitutions needed.

Use gluten-free pastas.

Use "Eggless Mayonnaise I" (see recipe)

Nutritional Analysis:
(for base recipe)
Serving Size = ½ cup

Calories (kcal):	162.0
Total Fat (g):	5.4
Saturated Fat (g):	0.8
Cholesterol (mg):	3.8
Carbohydrate (g):	24.8
Protein (g):	3.7
Sodium (mg):	149.6
Dietary Fiber (g):	1.3

Pasta Salad

Yields 4 cups

INGREDIENTS:

2 cups spiral pasta , cooked
1 cup broccoli flowerets
¼ cup black pitted olives, halved
½ red bell pepper diced
2 Tbsp. apple cider vinegar

3 oz. olive oil
1 Tbsp. water
½ tsp. chopped fresh garlic
¼ tsp. oregano
salt & pepper to taste

COMBINE pasta, broccoli, olives & red pepper in bowl.
TOSS to mix.
WHISK vinegar, oil & water together in separate bowl.
ADD garlic, oregano, salt & pepper.
WHISK to make dressing.
POUR over pasta mixture.
TOSS & chill.
TOSS again before serving.

No substitutions needed.

Use gluten-free pasta.

No substitutions needed.

Nutritional Analysis:
(for base recipe)
Serving Size = ½ cup

Calories (kcal):	95.8
Total Fat (g):	3.0
Saturated Fat (g):	0.5
Cholesterol (mg):	2.0
Carbohydrate (g):	16.7
Protein (g):	2.0
Sodium (mg):	14.0
Dietary Fiber (g):	2.3

Potato Salad

Yields 2 cups

INGREDIENTS:

2 cups red potatoes, cooked & cubed
3 - 4 Tbsp. mayonnaise
⅛ tsp. garlic powder
1 tsp. apple cider vinegar
paprika to taste

COMBINE ingredients in bowl.
SERVE.

No substitutions needed.

No substitutions needed.

Use "Eggless Mayonnaise I" (see recipe) & omit cider vinegar.

Nutritional Analysis:
(for base recipe)
Serving Size = ½ cup

Calories (kcal):	111.8
Total Fat (g):	4.5
Saturated Fat (g):	0.7
Cholesterol (mg):	3.3
Carbohydrate (g):	17.1
Protein (g):	1.8
Sodium (mg):	96.1
Dietary Fiber (g):	1.4

Zucchini Slaw

Yields 2 cups

INGREDIENTS:

2 cups shredded zucchini
1 cup shredded carrot
½ cup mayonnaise
1 tsp. sugar
¼ tsp. dill
1 tsp. cider vinegar
1 tsp. lemon juice
salt & pepper to taste

COMBINE ingredients in bowl.
TOSS to mix.
SERVE.

 No substitutions needed.

Use "Eggless Mayonnaise I" (see recipe)

Use "Eggless Mayonnaise I" (see recipe)

 Nutritional Analysis:
(for base recipe)
Serving Size = ½ cup

Calories (kcal):	139.7
Total Fat (g):	10.0
Saturated Fat (g):	1.5
Cholesterol (mg):	7.6
Carbohydrate (g):	12.9
Protein (g):	1.3
Sodium (mg):	259.5
Dietary Fiber (g):	1.6

Main Dishes

Bar-B-Qued Chicken Wings
Chicken Pot Pie
Chicken Strips
Eggplant Parmesan
Fish Sticks
Lasagna
Meatloaf Cannonballs
Oven Fried Chicken
Pizza Casserole
Pot Pie Crust
Spaghetti Sauce & Meatballs
Tuna Croquettes
Turkey Roll-ups

Bar-B-Qued Chicken Wings

yields 12 wings

INGREDIENTS:

12 chicken wings

⅛ tsp. paprika

⅛ tsp. salt

1 cup "Bar-B-Que Sauce"(see recipe)

PREHEAT oven to 350° F.
RINSE wings in cold water & pat dry.
SPRINKLE with paprika & salt.
BAKE for 10 minutes.
FLIP & bake for an additional 10 minutes.
BASTE with B-B-Que Sauce.
BROIL for 2 minutes.
FLIP wings & baste with additional sauce.
BROIL for 3 minutes or until done.
SERVE.

No substitutions needed.

No substitutions needed.

No substitutions needed.

Nutritional Analysis:
(for base recipe)
Serving Size = 2 wings

Calories (kcal):	265.9
Total Fat (g):	15.7
Saturated Fat (g):	4.4
Cholesterol (mg):	75.5
Carbohydrate (g):	12.6
Protein (g):	18.2
Sodium (mg):	170.6
Dietary Fiber (g):	0.3

Chicken Pot Pie

Yields two 7 inch deep dish pies

INGREDIENTS:

4 medium potatoes,
   peeled & cubed
1 lb. boneless chicken,
   cooked & cubed
2 cups frozen peas & carrots
2 ½ cups "Chicken Stock"
   (see recipe)
¼ cup potato starch
"Pot Pie Crust" (see recipe)

PREHEAT oven to 400° F.
BOIL potatoes until almost soft (approx. 5 minutes).
REMOVE from heat.
DRAIN potatoes & rinse with cold water to stop cooking process.
COMBINE potatoes, chicken, peas & carrots in bowl.
TOSS to mix.
ADD potato starch to ½ cup "Chicken Stock" & stir until completely dissolved.
SET aside.
HEAT remaining stock in medium sauce pan & bring to boil.
GRADUALLY add potato starch mixture to stock, stirring constantly, until a thick sauce is formed.
ADD sauce to chicken mixture & set aside.

TO MAKE PIE

PREPARE "Pot Pie Crust" (see recipe).
PRESS 1 dough ball into bottom & along sides of <u>ungreased</u> tin.
FILL prepared tin with half of chicken mixture & set aside.
PLACE 1 dough ball between 2 sheets of wax paper.
ROLL OUT to form 8 inch circle.
REMOVE top sheet of paper.
CAREFULLY FLIP crust onto top of pie.
SEAL EDGES with thumb prints.
CUT an "X" on top of pie to allow steam to escape during baking.
REPEAT procedure for second pie.
BAKE on foil lined cookie sheet for 30 minutes.
REMOVE from oven & let stand 5 minutes.
SERVE.

Nutritional Analysis:
   (for base recipe)
Serving Size = ⅓ pie

Calories (kcal):	494.4
Total Fat (g):	20.4
Saturated Fat (g):	4.6
Cholesterol (mg):	62.2
Carbohydrate (g):	53.8
Protein (g):	26.2
Sodium (mg):	214.3
Dietary Fiber (g):	5.5

No substitutions needed.

Chicken Strips

Yields 36 "strips"

INGREDIENTS:

2 cups "Seasoned Crumb Coating" (see recipe)
1 lb. boneless chicken breasts, cut into strips
¾ cup unsweetened apple juice
2 Tbsp. olive oil

PREHEAT oven to 350° F.
DREDGE chicken pieces in crumb coating.
DIP in apple juice.
DREDGE again in crumb coating.
PLACE on <u>ungreased</u> aluminum pan.
BRUSH with olive oil.
BAKE for 15 minutes.
TURN chicken strips over.
BRUSH with remaining oil.
BAKE for an additional 15 minutes.
SERVE.

No substitutions needed.

Use "Gluten-free Seasoned Crumb Coating"
(see recipe)

No substitutions needed.

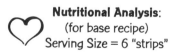

Nutritional Analysis:
(for base recipe)
Serving Size = 6 "strips"

Calories (kcal):	376.9
Total Fat (g):	15.2
Saturated Fat (g):	2.2
Cholesterol (mg):	43.9
Carbohydrate (g):	37.4
Protein (g):	21.8
Sodium (mg):	248.4
Dietary Fiber (g):	2.4

Eggplant Parmesan

Yields one 9 inch casserole

INGREDIENTS:

1 lb. eggplant, cut in ½ inch slices
salt
3 Tbsp. olive oil
1 cup "Italian Style Seasoned Crumb Coating" (see recipe)
1 ½ cups "Chunky Tomato Sauce"(see recipe)
6 oz. mozzarella cheese, shredded

PREHEAT oven to 350° F.
SPRINKLE both sides of eggplant slices with salt.
SPREAD slices in a single layer on a platter or board lined with paper towels.
COVER with paper towels & set aside for 20 - 30 minutes (to draw out bitterness & moisture).
PAT DRY.
LIGHTLY BRUSH eggplant on both sides with olive oil.
BAKE for approximately 8 minutes or until soft.
COOL.
COAT each slice in "Seasoned Crumb Coating".
POUR ¼ cup sauce into bottom of 9-inch baking dish.
PLACE a layer of eggplant slices over sauce.
SPOON a layer of sauce over eggplant.
REPEAT with remaining sauce & eggplant (alternating layers).
BAKE, uncovered, for 20 minutes.
SPRINKLE cheese over top of casserole.
BAKE for an additional 15 minutes or until cheese is slightly browned.
SERVE.

Use milk-free cheese.

Use "Gluten-free Seasoned Crumb Coating" (see recipe).

No substitutions needed.

Nutritional Analysis:
(for base recipe)
Serving Size = ⅙ casserole

Calories (kcal):	316.6
Total Fat (g):	18.2
Saturated Fat (g):	4.9
Cholesterol (mg):	16.2
Carbohydrate (g):	28.5
Protein (g):	12.0
Sodium (mg):	542.7
Dietary Fiber (g):	4.4

Page 73

Fish Sticks

Yields 18 "sticks"

INGREDIENTS:

½ lb. cod or whiting filet
2 Tbsp. lemon juice
¼ cup "Fish Style Seasoned Crumb Coating" (see recipe)
1 Tbsp. olive oil

PREHEAT oven to 350° F.
CUT fish into ½ inch strips.
ADD lemon juice.
STIR to coat.
DREDGE fish sticks in crumb coating.
PLACE on baking sheet.
BRUSH gently with olive oil.
BAKE until firm & golden (approx. 25 - 30 minutes).
SERVE.

 Serving Suggestion: Use tartar sauce as an accompaniment.

No substitutions needed.

Use "Gluten-free Seasoned Crumb Coating" (see recipe).

No substitutions needed.

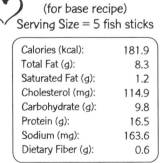

Nutritional Analysis:
(for base recipe)
Serving Size = 5 fish sticks

Calories (kcal):	181.9
Total Fat (g):	8.3
Saturated Fat (g):	1.2
Cholesterol (mg):	114.9
Carbohydrate (g):	9.8
Protein (g):	16.5
Sodium (mg):	163.6
Dietary Fiber (g):	0.6

Lasagna

Yields 1 casserole

INGREDIENTS:

16 oz. lasagna noodles
1 lb. ground beef
4 cups "Chunky Tomato Sauce" (see recipe)
16 oz. ricotta cheese
2 cups shredded mozzarella cheese

PREHEAT oven to 350° F.

COOK lasagna noodles according to package directions.

DRAIN & rinse in cold water.

PLACE noodles (in single layer) on wax paper to prevent sticking & set aside.

BROWN meat in skillet.

DRAIN excess fat.

COMBINE meat, 3 cups sauce & ricotta cheese.

SPREAD ½ cup remaining sauce on bottom of 13 x 9 inch baking dish.

LAYER dish with noodles (do not overlap), meat mixture & ½ cup mozzarella cheese.

REPEAT two times ending with a layer of noodles.

SPREAD remaining ⅓ cup of sauce over noodles.

SPRINKLE with remaining cheese.

COVER with foil.

BAKE for 30 minutes.

REMOVE foil & bake for additional 15 minutes.

SET for 10 minutes before slicing.

SERVE.

Substitute 16 oz. silken tofu for ricotta cheese.
Use milk-free mozzarella.

Use gluten-free noodles.

No substitutions needed.

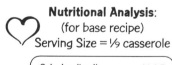

Nutritional Analysis:
(for base recipe)
Serving Size = ⅑ casserole

Calories (kcal):	414.7
Total Fat (g):	23.4
Saturated Fat (g):	10.5
Cholesterol (mg):	69.8
Carbohydrate (g):	27.8
Protein (g):	24.2
Sodium (mg):	382.2
Dietary Fiber (g):	3.3

Meatloaf Cannonballs

Yields 8 "cannonballs"

MEATLOAF INGREDIENTS:

1 ½ lb. ground beef

½ lb. ground chicken or turkey

½ cup "Bar-B-Que Sauce" (see recipe)

½ tsp. salt

⅛ tsp. black pepper

CANNONBALL CRUST:

6 medium potatoes, peeled,
    boiled & mashed

4 Tbsp. margarine

⅓ cup milk

½ tsp. salt

⅛ tsp. white pepper

paprika to taste

PREHEAT oven to 350° F.

MIX ingredients for meatloaf.

DIVIDE into 8 equal parts & place into individual muffin tins.

PLACE tins on cookie sheet to catch drippings.

BAKE for 25 minutes.

REMOVE from tins & set aside.

WHIP potatoes together with 2 Tbsp. margarine, milk, salt & pepper.

PRESS ½ cup potato mixture around each individual meatloaf, covering completely.

PLACE "cannonballs" on lightly greased cookie sheet.

MELT remaining margarine.

BRUSH each "cannonball" with melted margarine.

SPRINKLE with paprika.

BROIL for 3 minutes.

SERVE.

Use milk-free margarine &
a milk substitute.

No substitutions needed.

No substitutions needed.

Nutritional Analysis:
(for base recipe)
Serving Size = 1 "cannonball"

Calories (kcal):	429.3
Total Fat (g):	26.1
Saturated Fat (g):	9.1
Cholesterol (mg):	87.6
Carbohydrate (g):	25.6
Protein (g):	22.2
Sodium (mg):	471.5
Dietary Fiber (g):	2.0

Oven Fried Chicken

Yields 10 pieces

INGREDIENTS:

1 fryer chicken, cut into 10 pieces
1 cup crushed potato chips
½ cup all-purpose flour
1 tsp. salt
1 tsp. paprika
¼ cup melted margarine

PREHEAT oven to 350° F.
COMBINE potato chips, flour, salt & paprika & set aside.
BRUSH chicken pieces with melted margarine.
COAT in potato chip mixture.
BAKE for 60 minutes, turning chicken every 20 minutes.
SERVE.

Use milk-free margarine.

Substitute ½ cup brown rice flour for all-purpose flour.

No substitutions needed.

Nutritional Analysis:
(for base recipe)
Serving Size = 1 piece

Calories (kcal):	227.8
Total Fat (g):	14.9
Saturated Fat (g):	3.9
Cholesterol (mg):	53.8
Carbohydrate (g):	7.9
Protein (g):	15.0
Sodium (mg):	371.0
Dietary Fiber (g):	0.5

PiZZa Casserole

Yields 1 casserole

INGREDIENTS:

1 lb. thin spaghetti, cooked & drained
1 lb. ground beef
1 lb. mozzarella cheese, shredded
"Chunky Tomato Sauce" (see recipe)

PREHEAT oven to 350° F.

BROWN ground meat in skillet, stirring constantly.

DRAIN excess grease.

ADD "Chunky Tomato Sauce" & bring to boil.

SIMMER uncovered for 15 minutes, stirring occasionally.

GREASE a 14 inch deep dish pizza pan with oil.

LAYER ingredients starting with cooked noodles, then sauce & meat mixture.

SPRINKLE with cheese to cover.

BAKE 25 minutes or until ingredients are heated through & cheese has melted.

SERVE.

 Use milk-free cheese.

 Use gluten-free pasta.

No substitutions needed.

Nutritional Analysis:
(for base recipe)
Serving Size = ⅛ casserole

Calories (kcal):	461.7
Total Fat (g):	24.9
Saturated Fat (g):	11.4
Cholesterol (mg):	74.8
Carbohydrate (g):	29.2
Protein (g):	31.1
Sodium (mg):	565.3
Dietary Fiber (g):	3.7

Pot Pie Crust

Yields four 7 inch crusts

INGREDIENTS:

1 ½ cup brown rice flour
1 ½ cup garbanzo flour
2 tsp. sugar
½ cup margarine
½ cup vegetable shortening
6 Tbsp. ice water

PREHEAT oven to 400° F.
COMBINE flours, sugar, margarine & shortening.
ADD water, 1 Tbsp. at a time, to form dough.
DIVIDE dough into four equal parts.
ROLL OUT dough & bake according to pot pie recipe.

Use milk-free margarine.

No substitutions needed.

No substitutions needed.

Nutritional Analysis:
(for base recipe)
Serving Size = ⅙ crust

Calories (kcal):	252.0
Total Fat (g):	17.4
Saturated Fat (g):	3.8
Cholesterol (mg):	0
Carbohydrate (g):	22.0
Protein (g):	3.6
Sodium (mg):	92.0
Dietary Fiber (g):	2.0

Spaghetti Sauce & Meatballs

SPAGHETTI SAUCE:

1 medium onion, finely diced

1 large clove garlic, chopped

1 tsp. olive oil

26 oz. can chopped tomatoes

1 bay leaf

½ tsp. basil

½ tsp. oregano

⅛ tsp. pepper

Yields 3 cups sauce & 24 meatballs

SAUTE onion in olive oil over medium heat.

COOK until onion is translucent.

ADD garlic & cook for additional minute.

ADD tomatoes & seasonings.

STIR & bring to boil.

REDUCE heat.

COVER & simmer for 15 minutes, stirring occasionally.

MEATBALLS:

1 lb. ground turkey

1 tsp. onion powder

salt & pepper to taste

1 tsp. garlic powder

1 tsp. parsley flakes

PREHEAT oven to 325° F.

COMBINE all ingredients in a bowl.

ROLL mixture into 1 inch balls.

PLACE in baking dish & cover with sauce.

BAKE for 20 minutes.

SERVE.

Recipe Variation: Substitute your child's favorite ground meat!

No substitutions needed.

Nutritional Analysis:
(for base recipe)
Serving Size = 4 oz. sauce & 4 meatballs

SAUCE

Calories (kcal):	46.1
Total Fat (g):	1.3
Saturated Fat (g):	0.2
Cholesterol (mg):	0
Carbohydrate (g):	8.9
Protein (g):	1.7
Sodium (mg):	202.1
Dietary Fiber (g):	2.1

MEATBALLS

Calories (kcal):	115.6
Total Fat (g):	6.3
Saturated Fat (g):	1.7
Cholesterol (mg):	59.7
Carbohydrate (g):	0.7
Protein (g):	134.3
Sodium (mg):	97.5
Dietary Fiber (g):	0.1

Tuna Croquettes

Yields 15 croquettes

INGREDIENTS:
2 cups flaked tuna, drained
2 tsp. lemon juice
1 egg, beaten
1 tsp. parsley flakes
½ cup "Seasoned Crumb Coating" (see recipe)
vegetable oil for frying

TOSS tuna with lemon juice.
COMBINE with remaining ingredients.
FORM into tablespoon size patties.
FRY in ¼ inch oil until golden brown on each side.
DRAIN on paper towel.
SERVE with ketchup, cocktail sauce or tartar sauce.

 **Recipe Variation**: Use salmon instead of tuna.

 No substitutions needed.

Use "Gluten-free Seasoned Crumb Coating" (see recipe).

Substitute ¼ cup water mixed with
1 Tbsp. egg replacer for egg.

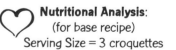 **Nutritional Analysis**:
(for base recipe)
Serving Size = 3 croquettes

Calories (kcal):	203.4
Total Fat (g):	6.6
Saturated Fat (g):	1.4
Cholesterol (mg):	80.6
Carbohydrate (g):	10.4
Protein (g):	24.0
Sodium (mg):	118.2
Dietary Fiber (g):	0.7

Turkey Roll-ups

Yields 6 "roll-ups"

INGREDIENTS:

6 turkey cutlets (4 oz. each)
2 cups unbaked "Stuffing"
   (see recipe)
½ tsp. paprika
½ tsp. garlic powder
1 tsp. parsley flakes
½ tsp. ground thyme
⅛ tsp. salt
1 Tbsp. margarine
½ cup orange juice
1 Tbsp. honey

PREHEAT oven to 350° F.
POUND cutlets to ¼ inch thickness.
PLACE 2 Tbsp. "Stuffing" towards one end of each cutlet.
ROLL UP jelly roll style.
PLACE, seam side down, in shallow roasting pan.
MIX paprika, garlic powder, parsley, thyme & salt together.
SPRINKLE roll-ups with ½ of seasoning mixture & set aside.
MELT margarine in small sauce pan.
ADD orange juice & honey & bring to boil.
REMOVE from heat.
BASTE roll-ups with orange juice mixture.
BAKE for 10 minutes.
FLIP.
SPRINKLE with remaining seasoning mixture.
BASTE.
BAKE for additional 10 minutes.
FLIP again & baste with remaining liquid.
BAKE for additional 5 minutes.
SERVE.

Use milk-free margarine.

Use "Gluten-free Stuffing" (see recipe) .

No substitutions needed.

Nutritional Analysis:
(for base recipe)
Serving Size = 1 "roll-up"

Calories (kcal):	243.4
Total Fat (g):	6.9
Saturated Fat (g):	1.8
Cholesterol (mg):	74.8
Carbohydrate (g):	17.6
Protein (g):	26.8
Sodium (mg):	352.5
Dietary Fiber (g):	1.4

Side Dishes

Noodle Pudding
Pizza Nests
Potato Pancakes
Potato Vegetable Patties
Stuffing
Sweet Potato Boats
Vegetable Tempura

Noodle Pudding

INGREDIENTS:

Yields one 8 x 8 inch casserole

1 box medium size noodles (8oz.)

2 Tbsp. melted margarine

2 eggs

½ cup plus 1 ½ tsp. sugar

1 tsp. vanilla

½ cup golden raisins

½ lb. canned fruit cocktail, drained

½ tsp. cinnamon

PREHEAT oven to 350°F.

GREASE 8 x 8 inch square pan.

COOK noodles according to directions on box, drain.

ADD margarine, eggs, ½ cup sugar & vanilla.

TOSS to mix.

POUR mixture into greased pan.

TOP with raisins & fruit cocktail.

MIX remaining sugar & cinnamon together in separate bowl.

SPRINKLE on top of fruit.

BAKE for 45 minutes.

SERVE room temperature or cold.

Use milk-free margarine.

Use gluten-free pasta.

Substitute 3 tsp. egg replacer mixed together with ¼ cup water for eggs. Use egg-free noodles.

Nutritional Analysis:
(for base recipe)
Serving Size = ⅑ of pudding

Calories (kcal):	152.8
Total Fat (g):	4.1
Saturated Fat (g):	0.9
Cholesterol (mg):	55.5
Carbohydrate (g):	27.0
Protein (g):	3.0
Sodium (mg):	47.5
Dietary Fiber (g):	0.9

PiZZa Nests

Yields 6 "nests"

INGREDIENTS:

8 oz. thin spaghetti, cooked & drained
1 cup "Chunky Tomato Sauce" (see recipe)
¾ cup shredded mozzarella cheese
1 small zucchini, sliced (or your favorite vegetable)
olive oil

PREHEAT oven to 350° F.
GREASE cookie sheet lightly with olive oil.
SCOOP ½ cup portions of cooked spaghetti onto cookie sheet to form "nests".
LAYER filling into nests in the following order: 1 Tbsp. cheese, 1 heaping Tbsp. sauce, 1 layer of zucchini, 1 Tbsp. cheese.
BAKE for 25 minutes.
SERVE.

Use milk-free cheese.

Use gluten-free pasta.

No substitutions needed.

Nutritional Analysis:
(for base recipe)
Serving Size = one 4oz. nest

Calories (kcal):	111.2
Total Fat (g):	3.1
Saturated Fat (g):	1.4
Cholesterol (mg):	6.4
Carbohydrate (g):	15.5
Protein (g):	6.0
Sodium (mg):	130.2
Dietary Fiber (g):	1.8

Potato Pancakes

Yields 12 pancakes

INGREDIENTS:

2 cups shredded potatoes, packed
½ Tbsp. lemon juice
2 eggs, beaten
2 Tbsp. potato starch flour
¾ tsp. salt
¼ tsp. white pepper
oil for frying

PLACE potatoes in a colander & press to remove excess liquid.

TOSS potatoes with lemon juice to keep from turning brown.

GRATE potatoes in food processor, turning on & off until potatoes are coarsely grated (be careful not to over process).

TRANSFER to bowl.

ADD eggs.

STIR to mix.

ADD potato starch flour, salt & pepper & stir to combine.

HEAT oil in skillet.

DROP potato mixture, by heaping tablespoon, into hot oil.

FRY until golden brown on both sides, flipping once.

DRAIN on paper towels.

SERVE immediately.

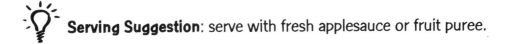

Serving Suggestion: serve with fresh applesauce or fruit puree.

No substitutions needed.

No substitutions needed.

Substitute 1 Tbsp. egg replacer mixed with ¼ cup water for eggs.

Nutritional Analysis:
(for base recipe)
Serving Size = 2 pancakes

Calories (kcal):	110.0
Total Fat (g):	4.0
Saturated Fat (g):	0.8
Cholesterol (mg):	70.8
Carbohydrate (g):	15.8
Protein (g):	3.1
Sodium (mg):	315.2
Dietary Fiber (g):	0.8

Potato Vegetable Patties

Yields 12 patties

INGREDIENTS:

1 Tbsp. olive oil
4 cloves garlic, finely diced
½ cup diced green peppers
¾ cup shredded zucchini
¾ cup shredded carrots
½ cup frozen chopped spinach, well drained

1 tsp. salt
¼ tsp. white pepper
1 cup mashed potatoes
1 cup mashed sweet potatoes
¼ cup potato starch flour
¼ cup "Seasoned Crumb Coating"
    (see recipe)

PREHEAT oven to 350° F.
HEAT oil in skillet.
ADD garlic & green peppers.
SAUTE for 2 minutes.
ADD zucchini & carrots.
CONTINUE to saute for an additional 3 minutes.
ADD spinach, salt & pepper.
COOK until vegetables are just softened.
REMOVE from heat & set aside.
COMBINE potatoes & sweet potatoes in bowl.
ADD vegetable mixture, potato starch flour & "Seasoned Crumb Coating".
MIX completely.
FORM into patties using ¼ cup measure.
PLACE on ungreased baking sheet.
BAKE for 10 minutes.
FLIP & bake for additional 10 minutes.
BROIL 1 minute on each side to brown.
SERVE.

No substitutions needed.

Use "Gluten-free Seasoned Crumb Coating" (see recipe).

No substitutions needed.

Nutritional Analysis:
(for base recipe)
Serving Size = 2 patties

Calories (kcal):	186.2
Total Fat (g):	3.8
Saturated Fat (g):	0.5
Cholesterol (mg):	0
Carbohydrate (g):	36.5
Protein (g):	3.0
Sodium (mg):	440.7
Dietary Fiber (g):	3.1

Stuffing

Yields 4 cups

INGREDIENTS:

16 slices bread, toasted with crust removed
½ cup celery, finely diced
¼ cup onion, finely diced
1 Tbsp. margarine
2 medium apples, grated

2 tsp. parsley flakes
1 tsp. dried thyme
½ tsp. salt
⅛ tsp. white pepper
½ cup "Chicken Stock"(see recipe)

PREHEAT oven to 350° F.
CUT bread into cubes & set aside in large bowl.
SAUTE celery & onion in margarine until soft.
ADD celery mixture & remaining ingredients to bread cubes.
TOSS until liquid is absorbed.
BAKE, uncovered, for 30 minutes.
SERVE.

 Serving Suggestion: Add your favorite combination of dried fruit, nuts, etc.

Use milk-free bread & milk-free margarine.

Use gluten-free bread.

No substitutions needed.

Nutritional Analysis:
(for base recipe)
Serving Size = ½ cup

Calories (kcal):	105.0
Total Fat (g):	2.5
Saturated Fat (g):	0.5
Cholesterol (mg):	1.6
Carbohydrate (g):	18.4
Protein (g):	2.7
Sodium (mg):	302.6
Dietary Fiber (g):	1.9

Sweet Potato Boats

Yields 16 "boats"

INGREDIENTS:

8 medium sweet potatoes
2 apples, peeled & cored
¼ cup orange juice
½ tsp. cinnamon

1 Tbsp. margarine
½ tsp. salt
1 egg
16 "Marshmallows" (see recipe)

PREHEAT oven to 375° F.

SLICE potatoes in half, lengthwise.

CUT small slit in center of potato.

BAKE for 45 minutes or until tender when pierced with knife (microwave according to your oven's directions to cut baking time considerably).

SCOOP out pulp of sweet potatoes being careful to leave skin intact.

ADD salt to pulp & set aside.

CUT apples into thin slices.

TOSS apples in orange juice & add cinnamon.

SAUTE apple mixture in margarine over medium heat, stirring constantly until apples are soft & liquid is absorbed.

ADD apple mixture to sweet potato pulp & process (or mash) until smooth.

BEAT egg into mixture.

FILL potato shells to rim.

BAKE on foil lined cookie sheets at 400° F for 30 minutes.

SLICE marshmallows in half.

TOP each potato half with 2 pieces of marshmallow.

BROIL until golden brown.

SERVE immediately.

Use milk-free margarine.

No substitutions needed.

Substitute 1 ½ tsp. egg replacer mixed with 2 Tbsp. of water for egg. Use egg-free "Marshmallows" (see recipe).

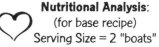

Nutritional Analysis:
(for base recipe)
Serving Size = 2 "boats"

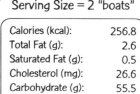

Calories (kcal):	256.8
Total Fat (g):	2.6
Saturated Fat (g):	0.5
Cholesterol (mg):	26.6
Carbohydrate (g):	55.5
Protein (g):	4.3
Sodium (mg):	226.6
Dietary Fiber (g):	4.6

Vegetable Tempura

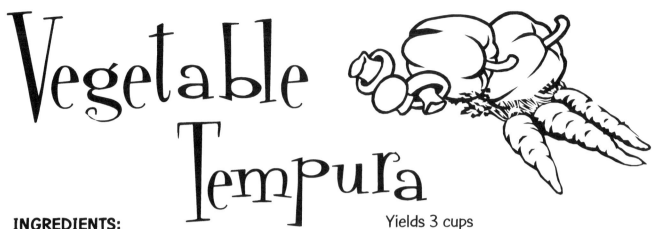

Yields 3 cups

INGREDIENTS:

1 egg
¾ cup ginger ale
¾ cup all-purpose flour
¼ cup corn flour
3 cups washed & cut-up vegetables[*]
    (sweet potatoes, zucchini,
    broccoli, carrots, etc.)
vegetable oil for deep frying

HEAT oil to 370° F.
MIX egg & ginger ale together.
SIFT flours together in a separate bowl.
ADD flour mixture to liquid.
BLEND until batter forms.
DIP vegetables, one at a time, into batter.
DEEP FRY, a few at a time, until golden brown.
   Be careful to keep oil temperature constant.
   Too hot will burn the vegetables.
   Too cold will make the tempura oily.
DRAIN on paper towels.
CLEAN oil of all crumbs, using spoon.
REPEAT with remaining vegetables.
SERVE immediately.

★ Some vegetables (sweet potatoes, carrots) may need to be blanched for 3 - 4 minutes prior to dipping in batter.

 Serving Suggestion: Use soy sauce for dipping vegetables.

 No substitutions needed.

Substitute ¾ cup sweet rice flour for all-purpose flour.

 Substitute 1 ½ tsp. egg replacer mixed together with 2 Tbsp. water for egg.

Nutritional Analysis:
(for base recipe)
Serving Size = ½ cup vegetables

Calories (kcal):	140.3
Total Fat (g):	1.5
Saturated Fat (g):	0.3
Cholesterol (mg):	35.4
Carbohydrate (g):	28.0
Protein (g):	4.0
Sodium (mg):	24.1
Dietary Fiber (g):	3.2

Sauces, Dips & Condiments

Bar-B-Que Sauce
Cheese Sauce
Chunky Tomato Sauce
Eggless Mayonnaise I
Eggless Mayonnaise II
Fruit Dressing
Guacamole
Pancake Paint
Seasoned Crumb Coating
Tartar Sauce

Bar-B-Que Sauce

Yields 1 ½ cups

INGREDIENTS:

½ cup tomato juice
½ cup tomato puree
¼ cup light corn syrup
2 Tbsp. cider vinegar
¼ cup apricot spreadable fruit
1 Tbsp. lemon juice
2 Tbsp. brown sugar
¼ tsp. celery seed
1 clove garlic, pressed
¼ tsp. paprika
⅛ tsp. chili powder
1 Tbsp. molasses

COMBINE ingredients in medium sauce pan.
HEAT to boil.
REDUCE heat & simmer for 10 minutes, stirring occasionally.
COOL completely before using.
REFRIGERATE in an airtight container.

No substitutions needed.

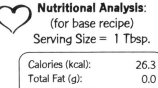

Nutritional Analysis:
(for base recipe)
Serving Size = 1 Tbsp.

Calories (kcal):	26.3
Total Fat (g):	0.0
Saturated Fat (g):	0.0
Cholesterol (mg):	0.0
Carbohydrate (g):	6.8
Protein (g):	0.1
Sodium (mg):	27.6
Dietary Fiber (g):	0.2

Cheese Sauce

Yields 2 cups

INGREDIENTS:

4 Tbsp. corn starch
2 cups "Chicken Stock" (see recipe)
⅛ tsp. white pepper
1 cup shredded American cheese

ADD cornstarch to ¼ cup chicken stock.

STIR until completely dissolved & set aside.

COMBINE remaining 1¾ cups stock with pepper in a medium saucepan.

HEAT to boil.

REDUCE heat.

GRADUALLY ADD cornstarch mixture to stock, stirring constantly, until a thick sauce is formed.

ADD cheese, stirring constantly, until cheese has melted & sauce is smooth.

SERVE.

Use milk-free cheese.

No substitutions needed.

No substitutions needed.

Nutritional Analysis:
(for base recipe)
Serving Size = 2 Tbsp.

Calories (kcal):	36.2
Total Fat (g):	1.9
Saturated Fat (g):	1.1
Cholesterol (mg):	8.0
Carbohydrate (g):	2.6
Protein (g):	2.1
Sodium (mg):	87.5
Dietary Fiber (g):	0.2

Chunky Tomato Sauce

Yields 4 cups

INGREDIENTS:

1 medium onion, chopped
1 Tbsp. olive oil
2 cloves garlic, finely chopped
26 oz. can chopped tomatoes
1 bay leaf
½ tsp. oregano
1 can (6oz.) tomato paste
salt & pepper to taste

SAUTE onion in oil, over medium heat, until soft.
ADD garlic & saute for 2 minutes.
ADD chopped tomatoes, bring to boil.
ADD bay leaf, oregano, tomato paste, salt & pepper.
SIMMER for 15 minutes, stirring occasionally.
REFRIGERATE in airtight container or freeze.

No substitutions needed.

Nutritional Analysis:
(for base recipe)
Serving Size = 4 oz.

Calories (kcal):	67.1
Total Fat (g):	2.3
Saturated Fat (g):	0.3
Cholesterol (mg):	0
Carbohydrate (g):	11.7
Protein (g):	2.2
Sodium (mg):	184.9
Dietary Fiber (g):	2.7

Eggless Mayonnaise 1

Yields 1 ¼ cups

INGREDIENTS:

1 10.5 oz. pkg. silken tofu, drained & crumbled
1 ½ Tbsp. lemon juice
1 Tbsp. rice vinegar
2 tsp. sugar
½ tsp. salt
¼ tsp. dry mustard
2 Tbsp. safflower oil

COMBINE first six ingredients in food processor or blender.
ADD oil while processor is running.
BLEND until smooth & creamy.
REFRIGERATE in covered container.

Recipe Variation: Add up to 2 Tbsp. dried herbs during processing to make different dressings!

No substitutions needed.

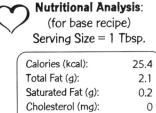

Nutritional Analysis:
(for base recipe)
Serving Size = 1 Tbsp.

Calories (kcal):	25.4
Total Fat (g):	2.1
Saturated Fat (g):	0.2
Cholesterol (mg):	0
Carbohydrate (g):	0.8
Protein (g):	1.2
Sodium (mg):	59.4
Dietary Fiber (g):	0.2

Eggless Mayonnaise II

Yields 1 cup

INGREDIENTS:

2 Tbsp. rice vinegar
4 Tbsp. lemon juice
1 cup hot mashed potatoes
3 tsp. sugar
½ tsp. dry mustard
¾ cup safflower oil

COMBINE first five ingredients in blender or food processor.
ADD oil while processor is running.
BLEND until smooth.
REFRIGERATE mixture (it will thicken as it cools).
STIR before serving as mixture may separate.

No substitutions needed.

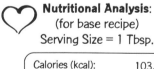

Nutritional Analysis:
(for base recipe)
Serving Size = 1 Tbsp.

Calories (kcal):	103.1
Total Fat (g):	10.3
Saturated Fat (g):	0.9
Cholesterol (mg):	0
Carbohydrate (g):	3.0
Protein (g):	0.2
Sodium (mg):	1.3
Dietary Fiber (g):	0.2

Fruit Dressing

Yields 1 cup

INGREDIENTS:

1 cup plain yogurt
¼ cup apricot spreadable fruit
¼ tsp. vanilla

COMBINE ingredients in blender until smooth.
REFRIGERATE in airtight container.
SERVE chilled.

Substitute ¾ cup silken tofu for yogurt. Add 2 Tbsp. orange juice,
2 Tbsp. water & 2 tsp. lemon juice. Increase vanilla to ½ tsp.

No substitutions needed.

No substitutions needed.

Nutritional Analysis:
(for base recipe)
Serving Size = 1 Tbsp.

Calories (kcal):	21.7
Total Fat (g):	0.5
Saturated Fat (g):	0.3
Cholesterol (mg):	1.9
Carbohydrate (g):	3.9
Protein (g):	0.6
Sodium (mg):	9.1
Dietary Fiber (g):	0.1

Guacamole

Yields 1 ½ cups

INGREDIENTS:
1 avocado, peeled & pitted
¼ lemon, squeezed
½ tsp. salt
⅛ tsp. white pepper
1 clove garlic, finely chopped
1 cup cold mashed potatoes

MASH avocado using fork or potato masher (texture should be slightly lumpy).
ADD lemon, salt, pepper & garlic.
TOSS lightly & set aside.
PUREE potatoes in food processor to remove all lumps, being careful not to over process.
FOLD potatoes into avocado mixture.
REFRIGERATE until ready to serve.

 Serving Suggestion: Serve with "Tortilla Chips" (see recipe)

No substitutions needed.

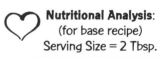 **Nutritional Analysis**:
(for base recipe)
Serving Size = 2 Tbsp.

Calories (kcal):	38.9
Total Fat (g):	2.6
Saturated Fat (g):	0.4
Cholesterol (mg):	0
Carbohydrate (g):	4.1
Protein (g):	0.6
Sodium (mg):	99.3
Dietary Fiber (g):	1.1

Pancake Paint

Each recipe yields 1 cup

ORANGE:
1 cup dried apricots
water

> **PUT** dried apricots in small pot.
> **ADD** enough water to cover fruit & bring to boil.
> **SIMMER** until liquid is almost absorbed (approximately 15 minutes).
> **PUREE** in food processor with ½ cup warm water until smooth.
> **SERVE**.

WHITE:
2 bananas
2 Tbsp. orange juice

> **PUREE** bananas with orange juice until smooth.
> **SERVE**.

RED:
1 pear, peeled & cored
1 cup cherries (frozen or fresh)
water

> **SIMMER** pear in enough water to cover fruit until soft (approximately 20 - 30 minutes).
> **DISCARD** liquid.
> **PUREE** pear & cherries until smooth.
> **SERVE**.

BLUE:
2 cups blueberries
 (frozen or fresh)

> **PUREE** blueberries until smooth.
> **SERVE**.

Serving Suggestion: Use in place of maple syrup, chocolate syrup or other toppings.

No substitutions needed.

Nutritional Analysis:
(for base recipe)
Serving Size = 1 oz.

	ORANGE	WHITE	RED	BLUE
Calories (kcal):	38.7	28.0	25.3	20.3
Total Fat (g):	0.1	0.1	0.3	0.1
Saturated Fat (g):	0	0.1	0	0
Cholesterol (mg):	0	0	0	0
Carbohydrate (g):	10.0	7.0	6.1	5.1
Protein (g):	0.6	0.3	0.3	0.2
Sodium (mg):	2.1	0.3	0	2.2
Dietary Fiber (g):	1.5	0.7	0.9	1.0

Seasoned Crumb Coating

Yields 2 cups

INGREDIENTS:

1 ¼ cups all-purpose flour
¾ cup white corn meal
1 tsp. paprika
½ tsp. salt
1¾ tsp. onion powder
1¾ tsp. garlic powder
½ tsp. oregano
½ tsp. basil
1 tsp. parsley
4 Tbsp. olive oil

COMBINE dry ingredients in food processor.
ADD olive oil, 1 Tbsp. at a time, while processor is running.
CONTINUE to process until oil is completely mixed in.
STORE in airtight container.

 **Recipe Variations**:

Fish Coating: Omit basil & oregano. Add ¾ tsp. thyme & ¼ cup sesame seeds.
Cajun Coating: Add chili powder to taste.
Indian Coating: Add curry powder to taste.

No substitutions needed.

Substitute ¾ cup brown rice flour & ½ cup chick pea flour for all-purpose flour.

No substitutions needed.

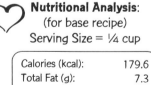 **Nutritional Analysis**:
(for base recipe)
Serving Size = ¼ cup

Calories (kcal):	179.6
Total Fat (g):	7.3
Saturated Fat (g):	1.0
Cholesterol (mg):	.0
Carbohydrate (g):	25.3
Protein (g):	3.2
Sodium (mg):	148.7
Dietary Fiber (g):	1.7

Tartar Sauce

Yields 1 cup

INGREDIENTS:

1 cup "Eggless Mayonnaise I" (see recipe)
2 Tbsp. pickle relish
¼ tsp. garlic powder

WHISK ingredients together.
CHILL.
SERVE.

No substitutions needed.

Use gluten-free relish.

No substitutions needed.

Nutritional Analysis:
(for base recipe)
Serving Size = 1 Tbsp.

Calories (kcal):	28.0
Total Fat (g):	2.1
Saturated Fat (g):	0.2
Cholesterol (mg):	0
Carbohydrate (g):	1.5
Protein (g):	1.2
Sodium (mg):	74.6
Dietary Fiber (g):	0.2

Desserts

Apple Crisp
Apple Filling
Apple Pie
Chocolate Cake
Chocolate Cupcakes
Chocolate Pudding
Cookie Pizza
Fruit Ravioli
Homemade Pie Crust
Jelly Roll Cake
Orange Sherbet
Peach Cobbler
Quick Rice Pudding
Vanilla Gelato
Waffle Ice Cream sandwiches
White Cake

Apple Crisp

Yields 4½ cups

FILLING:
4 apples, peeled, cored & chunked
2 tsp. lemon juice
½ cup sugar
2 Tbsp. brown sugar
1 tsp. vanilla
1 tsp. cinnamon
2 Tbsp. all-purpose flour

TOPPING:
¾ cup almonds
⅔ cup brown sugar
⅓ cup all-purpose flour
⅓ cup margarine

PREHEAT oven to 350° F.
COMBINE all ingredients for filling.
POUR into 8 or 9 inch glass baking dish.
MICROWAVE on high for 4 minutes.
MIX together almonds, brown sugar & flour in food processor.
PROCESS using on/off switch until coarsely chopped.
ADD margarine & combine until crumbly to form topping.
COVER apple mixture with topping.
BAKE on cookie sheet for 25 minutes.
COOL for 15 minutes.
SERVE, scooped warm.

 Serving Suggestion: top with whipped cream or vanilla ice cream.

Use milk-free margarine.

Substitute equal parts cornstarch for flour in filling & topping.

No substitutions needed.

Nutritional Analysis:
(for base recipe)
Serving Size = ½ cup

Calories (kcal):	283.9
Total Fat (g):	13.4
Saturated Fat (g):	2.0
Cholesterol (mg):	0
Carbohydrate (g):	40.4
Protein (g):	3.3
Sodium (mg):	85.6
Dietary Fiber (g):	2.8

Apple Filling

Yields 1 cup

INGREDIENTS:

2 macintosh apples, peeled, cored & diced
1 tsp. lemon juice
1 Tbsp. margarine
1 Tbsp. light brown sugar
1 Tbsp. sugar
⅛ tsp. cinnamon
pinch of salt
2 tsp. cornstarch

TOSS apples in lemon juice.
SAUTE apples in margarine until soft (approximately 5 minutes).
REMOVE from heat & add remaining ingredients in order.
SERVE warm or cold.

 Serving Suggestion: use in your favorite pie recipe.

Use milk-free margarine.

No substitutions needed.

No substitutions needed.

Nutritional Analysis:
(for base recipe)
Serving Size = ¼ cup

Calories (kcal):	88.5
Total Fat (g):	3.0
Saturated Fat (g):	0.6
Cholesterol (mg):	0
Carbohydrate (g):	16.4
Protein (g):	0.1
Sodium (mg):	40.2
Dietary Fiber (g):	1.3

Apple Pie

Yields one 9 inch apple pie

INGREDIENTS:

"Homemade Pie Crust" (see recipe)
5 large apples, peeled & cored
2 tsp. lemon juice
½ cup plus 3 tsp. sugar
2 Tbsp. brown sugar
1 tsp. vanilla
1 ¼ tsp. cinnamon
2 Tbsp. all-purpose flour
1 Tbsp. margarine

FILLING:

CUT apples into chunks.
COMBINE apple chunks with lemon juice.
ADD ½ cup sugar, brown sugar, vanilla,
1 tsp. cinnamon & flour.
STIR to coat.

PREHEAT oven to 450° F.
ROLL OUT 1 portion of dough on lightly floured board ¼ inch thick to cover 9 inch pie shell.
PLACE in pie tin, removing excess dough from edge of pan.
PAT down dough to fit pan.
PRICK bottom with fork.
FILL with apple mixture.
DOT with margarine.
ROLL OUT second portion of dough to cover pie.
TOP pie with crust, sealing edges with tines of fork or thumb.
PRICK top with fork to allow air to escape.
MIX remaining cinnamon & sugar in separate bowl.
PAT crust with water.
SPRINKLE crust with cinnamon & sugar mixture.
BAKE on cookie sheet for 10 minutes.
REDUCE heat to 350° F & bake for additional 30 - 35 minutes or until golden brown.
SERVE warm or cold.

Use milk-free margarine.

Substitute 2 Tbsp. cornstarch for all-purpose flour in filling. Use gluten-free pie crust.

No substitutions needed.

Nutritional Analysis:
(for base recipe)
Serving Size = ⅒ of pie

Calories (kcal):	258.7
Total Fat (g):	11.2
Saturated Fat (g):	2.3
Cholesterol (mg):	0
Carbohydrate (g):	38.3
Protein (g):	2.2
Sodium (mg):	63.0
Dietary Fiber (g):	1.9

Chocolate Cake

Yields two 9 inch layer cakes

INGREDIENTS:

1 ½ cups all-purpose flour
½ tsp. salt
2 tsp. baking powder
½ tsp. baking soda
½ cup unsweetened cocoa
½ cup milk

2 eggs
1 cup sugar
½ cup water
6 Tbsp. safflower oil
2 tsp. vanilla

PREHEAT oven to 350° F.
GREASE two 9-inch round cake pans & set aside.
COMBINE flour, salt, baking powder, baking soda & cocoa.
ADD milk & beat with mixer until liquid is absorbed.
BEAT remaining ingredients in separate bowl.
ADD to flour mixture & beat until smooth.
POUR into prepared pans.
BAKE for 30 minutes.
COOL on rack.
FROST with desired frosting.
SERVE.

Use ½ cup milk substitute (goat, soy, nut, etc.).

Substitute ¾ cup brown rice flour plus ½ cup potato starch for all-purpose flour. Add 1 additional Tbsp. oil.

Substitute 3 tsp. egg replacer mixed together with 4 Tbsp. water for egg.

Nutritional Analysis:
(for base recipe)
Serving Size = ⅒ slice of cake

Calories (kcal):	253.6
Total Fat (g):	10.4
Saturated Fat (g):	1.7
Cholesterol (mg):	44.2
Carbohydrate (g):	37.7
Protein (g):	4.4
Sodium (mg):	296.8
Dietary Fiber (g):	1.9

Chocolate Cupcakes

Yields 24 cupcakes

INGREDIENTS:

3 cups all-purpose flour
1 ½ cups sugar
6 Tbsp. unsweetened cocoa
2 tsp. baking soda
2 tsp. baking powder

½ tsp. salt
½ cup plus 2 Tbsp. safflower oil
2 tsp. vanilla
2 tsp. lemon juice
2 cups warm water
"Chocolate Glaze" (see recipe)

PREHEAT oven to 350° F.

LINE cupcake tins with bake cups or use <u>ungreased</u> tins.

COMBINE flour, sugar, cocoa, baking soda, baking powder & salt.

ADD oil, vanilla, lemon juice & water.

BEAT until smooth.

POUR batter into prepared tins, approximately ⅔ full.

BAKE for 18 - 20 minutes.

COOL.

DIP top of cupcakes in "Chocolate Glaze".

SERVE.

Recipe Variation: recipe can be used to make two 9 inch layer cakes.

 No substitutions needed.

 Substitute 2 cups brown rice flour, ⅔ cup potato starch & ⅓ cup tapioca flour for all-purpose flour. Add 1 tsp. xanthan gum.

 No substitutions needed.

Nutritional Analysis:
(for base recipe)
Serving Size = 1 cupcake

Calories (kcal):	160.0
Total Fat (g):	6.0
Saturated Fat (g):	0.7
Cholesterol (mg):	0
Carbohydrate (g):	25.4
Protein (g):	1.9
Sodium (mg):	195.6
Dietary Fiber (g):	0.9

Chocolate Pudding

Yields 4 cups

INGREDIENTS:

2 ¼ cups milk (room temperature)
⅓ cup sugar
3 Tbsp. cornstarch
1 oz. unsweetened chocolate
1 tsp. vanilla

MIX together ¼ cup milk, sugar & cornstarch & set aside.

HEAT chocolate & remaining milk over medium-high flame until it just begins to boil.

REDUCE heat to simmer.

ADD cornstarch mixture, stirring constantly until pudding thickens.

REMOVE from heat.

STIR in vanilla.

SPOON into individual cups.

CHILL until set.

SERVE.

 Use milk substitute.

 No substitutions needed.

No substitutions needed.

Nutritional Analysis:
(for base recipe)
Serving Size = ½ cup

Calories (kcal):	215.8
Total Fat (g):	9.0
Saturated Fat (g):	5.4
Cholesterol (mg):	19.6
Carbohydrate (g):	30.7
Protein (g):	5.3
Sodium (mg):	68.8
Dietary Fiber (g):	1.2

Cookie Pizza

Yields 1 pizza

INGREDIENTS:

"Sugar Cookies" dough (see recipe), chilled
1 ½ cups assorted fruit*, sliced thin
12 oz. cherry preserves
3 Tbsp. water
½ cup mini marshmallows

★ When using fruit that turns brown easily (apples, bananas, etc.),
lightly toss in lemon juice.

PREHEAT oven to 350° F.
PRESS dough evenly into 14-inch pizza pan, using lightly floured hands.
BAKE 10 - 12 minutes, until slightly golden.
COOL pan on rack.
COMBINE preserves & water in a small saucepan.
HEAT, stirring constantly, until completely blended.
REMOVE from heat & set aside.
ARRANGE fruit on "crust".
SPOON preserve mixture over entire pizza.
SPRINKLE with marshmallows.
BROIL for 30 seconds.
CHILL until glaze sets.
SERVE.

 Use milk-free "Sugar Cookies" dough (see recipe).

 Use gluten-free "Sugar Cookies" dough (see recipe)
& gluten-free "Marshmallows" (see recipe).

 Use egg-free "Sugar Cookies" dough (see recipe).

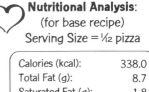 **Nutritional Analysis**:
(for base recipe)
Serving Size = ½ pizza

Calories (kcal):	338.0
Total Fat (g):	8.7
Saturated Fat (g):	1.8
Cholesterol (mg):	35.4
Carbohydrate (g):	62.6
Protein (g):	4.2
Sodium (mg):	259.9
Dietary Fiber (g):	1.3

Fruit Ravioli

Yields 12 raviolis

INGREDIENTS:

1 ½ cups all-purpose flour
¼ cup margarine
¼ cup vegetable shortening
1 Tbsp. sugar
½ tsp. cinnamon

3 - 4 Tbsp. ice water
1 cup pie filling
oil for frying
cinnamon & sugar mixture★

★ cinnamon & sugar = mix ½ cup sugar with 1 Tbsp. cinnamon

COMBINE flour, margarine, shortening, sugar & cinnamon in bowl.
ADD ice water, 1 Tbsp. at a time, to form dough.
WRAP in wax paper & freeze for 20 minutes.
ROLL OUT to ¼ inch thickness.
CUT into 2 inch squares or use ravioli cutter.
FILL half of the squares with heaping tsp. of filling.
MOISTEN edges slightly with water.
TOP with remaining halves.
SEAL using tines of fork.
DEEP FRY until golden brown.
PAT DRY on paper towel.
ROLL in cinnamon & sugar mixture.
SERVE warm.

Use milk-free margarine.

Substitute ¼ cup tapioca flour, ¼ cup corn starch, 2 Tbsp. potato flour, ½ cup brown rice flour & ¾ tsp. xanthan gum for all-purpose flour.
Substitute 1 egg & 1 tsp. apple cider vinegar for water.

No substitutions needed.

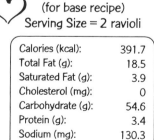

Nutritional Analysis:
(for base recipe)
Serving Size = 2 ravioli

Calories (kcal):	391.7
Total Fat (g):	18.5
Saturated Fat (g):	3.9
Cholesterol (mg):	0
Carbohydrate (g):	54.6
Protein (g):	3.4
Sodium (mg):	130.3
Dietary Fiber (g):	2.4

Homemade Pie Crust

Yields two 9 inch crusts

INGREDIENTS:

3 cups all-purpose flour
½ cup margarine
½ cup vegetable shortening
6 - 8 Tbsp. ice water

COMBINE flour, margarine & vegetable shortening in bowl.
ADD ice water, 1 Tbsp. at a time to form stiff dough.
DIVIDE into two equal portions.
FREEZE in wax paper for 20 minutes.
ROLL OUT dough according to pie recipe.

 Use milk-free margarine.

 Substitute ½ cup tapioca flour, ½ cup cornstarch,
¼ cup potato flour, 1 cup brown rice flour & 1 ½ tsp
xanthan gum for all-purpose flour. Add 2 tsp. sugar (optional).
Substitute 1 egg, 2 tsp. apple cider vinegar &
4 Tbsp. ice water for water.

 No substitutions needed.

Nutritional Analysis:
(for base recipe)
Serving Size = ¹⁄₁₀ of crust

Calories (kcal):	153.7
Total Fat (g):	9.9
Saturated Fat (g):	2.1
Cholesterol (mg):	0
Carbohydrate (g):	14.2
Protein (g):	2.0
Sodium (mg):	61.8
Dietary Fiber (g):	0.5

Jelly Roll Cake

Yields 1 cake

INGREDIENTS:

¾ cup all-purpose flour
1 tsp. baking powder
1 tsp. dried lemon peel
¼ tsp. salt
4 eggs, separated
1 tsp. vanilla
½ tsp. cream of tartar
⅔ cup sugar
confectioner's sugar
12 oz. fruit preserves
"Chocolate Glaze" (see recipe)

 Recipe Variation:
Fill with your favorite
ice cream, frosting, etc.

PREHEAT oven to 375° F.
GREASE jelly roll pan.
LINE with wax paper & grease again.
MIX flour, baking powder, lemon peel & salt in a small bowl & set aside.
BEAT egg yolks with vanilla until creamy & set aside.
WHIP egg whites in a separate bowl until frothy.
ADD cream of tartar & 1 Tbsp. sugar.
BEAT until stiff peaks form.
FOLD in egg yolks.
GRADUALLY ADD remaining sugar.
FOLD in flour mixture.
POUR into prepared pan.
BAKE 12 - 15 minutes.
DUST dish towel with confectioner's sugar while cake is baking.
REMOVE cake from oven & invert on towel.
PEEL off wax paper & trim edges of cake with sharp knife.
CAREFULLY ROLL cake in towel, working quickly.
COOL.
UNROLL cake when cooled completely.
SPREAD preserves evenly on cake.
ROLL to form log.
ARRANGE on platter, seam side down.
FROST with "Chocolate Glaze".
REFRIGERATE until set.
SERVE.

No substitutions needed.

Substitute ½ cup sweet rice flour & ¼ cup potato flour for all-purpose flour.

Substitute 2 Tbsp. egg replacer mixed with ¼ cup water for egg yolks & 2 Tbsp. egg replacer mixed with ½ cup water for egg whites. Bake 15 -18 minutes.

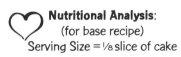 **Nutritional Analysis**:
(for base recipe)
Serving Size = ⅛ slice of cake

Calories (kcal):	366.3
Total Fat (g):	11.6
Saturated Fat (g):	4.0
Cholesterol (mg):	106.3
Carbohydrate (g):	64.5
Protein (g):	5.2
Sodium (mg):	243.7
Dietary Fiber (g):	1.6

Orange Sherbet

Yields 3 cups

INGREDIENTS:

1 orange
½ cup sugar
¾ cup orange juice
¾ cup water
½ cup plain yogurt
½ tsp. vanilla

PEEL orange, cutting through flesh.
REMOVE segments separately, without pith.
ADD 1 Tbsp. sugar & blend until smooth.
ADD enough orange juice to make 1 cup liquid.
BLEND.
ADD water & remaining sugar.
BLEND until smooth.
FREEZE to slushy consistency.
POUR into blender.
ADD yogurt & vanilla.
BLEND until smooth.
FREEZE until firm.
SERVE.

 **Serving Suggestion:** Cut orange in half. Scoop out inside. Fill with sherbet.

Substitute silken tofu for yogurt.

No substitutions needed.

No substitutions needed.

Nutritional Analysis:
(for base recipe)
Serving Size = ½ cup

Calories (kcal):	102.6
Total Fat (g):	0.8
Saturated Fat (g):	0.4
Cholesterol (mg):	2.6
Carbohydrate (g):	22.5
Protein (g):	1.2
Sodium (mg):	10.9
Dietary Fiber (g):	0.6

Peach Cobbler

Yields 4 cups

INGREDIENTS:

4 cups canned, sliced peaches
    (in their own juice)
4 tsp. cornstarch
1 ½ tsp. vanilla
¼ cup apricot spreadable fruit
1 Tbsp. brown sugar
¼ tsp. cinnamon
¾ cup plus 2 Tbsp.
    all-purpose flour
¼ tsp. salt
1 tsp. baking powder
½ tsp. baking soda
1 Tbsp. sugar
1 ½ Tbsp. margarine, chilled
1 Tbsp. vegetable shortening
⅓ cup water

PREHEAT oven to 425° F.
DRAIN peaches & place in 8 x 8 inch pan, reserving ½ cup juice.
ADD peach juice to cornstarch.
WHISK until smooth.
ADD 1 tsp. vanilla.
HEAT over low flame, whisking constantly until thick.
REMOVE from heat.
ADD spreadable fruit & stir until smooth.
POUR warm mixture over peaches & toss to coat.
COMBINE brown sugar & cinnamon.
SPRINKLE evenly over peach mixture & set aside.
SIFT together flour, salt, baking powder, baking soda & sugar in bowl.
CUT IN margarine & shortening using pastry blender or two knives,
until consistency of coarse corn meal.
FORM well in center of mixture.
ADD water & remaining vanilla.
MIX to form dough.
SPOON dough evenly over peaches.
MOISTEN fingers with water & smooth out top.
BAKE for 20 minutes or until golden brown.
SERVE warm

Use milk-free margarine.

Substitute ½ cup brown rice flour & 6 Tbsp. potato starch flour for all-purpose flour. Increase baking powder to 2 tsp. Add 1 tsp. xanthan gum to dry flour mixture.
Substitute 5 Tbsp. club soda for water. Spread 1 Tbsp. melted margarine over dough mixture before baking.

No substitutions needed.

Nutritional Analysis:
  (for base recipe)
Serving Size = ½ cup

Calories (kcal):	177.7
Total Fat (g):	3.9
Saturated Fat (g):	0.8
Cholesterol (mg):	0
Carbohydrate (g):	34.5
Protein (g):	2.2
Sodium (mg):	243.7
Dietary Fiber (g):	2.0

Quick Rice Pudding

Yields 4 cups

INGREDIENTS:

2 ¼ cups milk
3 Tbsp. cornstarch
½ cup sugar
2 tsp. vanilla
2 cups cooked rice
cinnamon, to taste

MIX ¼ cup milk, cornstarch & sugar & set aside.
HEAT remaining milk over medium-high flame until it just begins to boil.
REDUCE heat to simmer.
ADD cornstarch mixture, stirring constantly until pudding thickens.
REMOVE from heat.
STIR in vanilla.
ADD rice & mix until blended.
SPOON into individual cups.
SPRINKLE with cinnamon.
CHILL.
SERVE.

Use milk substitute.

No substitutions needed.

No substitutions needed.

Nutritional Analysis:
(for base recipe)
Serving Size = ½ cup

Calories (kcal):	168.1
Total Fat (g):	2.6
Saturated Fat (g):	1.6
Cholesterol (mg):	9.8
Carbohydrate (g):	32.0
Protein (g):	3.4
Sodium (mg):	34.0
Dietary Fiber (g):	0.2

Vanilla Gelato

Yields 3 cups

INGREDIENTS:

3 cups milk
¾ cup sugar
1 ½ tsp. vanilla

COOK 1 cup milk & sugar over low heat, stirring to dissolve.
REMOVE from heat.
ADD vanilla & remaining milk.
REFRIGERATE until cold.
POUR into ice cream maker & freeze according to manufacturer's directions.
SERVE.

FREEZER METHOD:

POUR into ice cube trays.
FREEZE until almost firm.
BLEND until smooth.
REFREEZE until firm.
SERVE.

 Use milk substitute.

 No substitutions needed.

 No substitutions needed.

Nutritional Analysis:
(for base recipe)
Serving Size = ½ cup

Calories (kcal):	175.6
Total Fat (g):	4.1
Saturated Fat (g):	2.5
Cholesterol (mg):	16.6
Carbohydrate (g):	31.0
Protein (g):	4.0
Sodium (mg):	60.1
Dietary Fiber (g):	0

Waffle Ice Cream Sandwiches

Yields 8 sandwiches

INGREDIENTS:

8 frozen "Waffles" (see recipe)
1 pint vanilla ice cream, softened
"Chocolate Glaze" (see recipe)

CUT waffles in half, lengthwise.
SPREAD ¼ cup ice cream over ½ of waffle.
TOP with remaining half to form sandwich.
PLACE on cookie sheet lined with wax paper.
REPEAT with remaining waffles.
FREEZE until firm.
DIP each sandwich into "Chocolate Glaze" (approximately ¾) to coat.
FREEZE until chocolate hardens.
SERVE.

 Serving Suggestion: dip sandwich in sprinkles or nuts before chocolate hardens.

 Use milk-free "Waffles" &"Chocolate Glaze".
Substitute your favorite dairy-free frozen dessert for ice cream.

 Use gluten-free "Waffles" & "Chocolate Glaze".

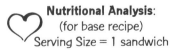

 Use egg-free "Waffles".

Nutritional Analysis:
(for base recipe)
Serving Size = 1 sandwich

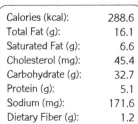

Calories (kcal):	288.6
Total Fat (g):	16.1
Saturated Fat (g):	6.6
Cholesterol (mg):	45.4
Carbohydrate (g):	32.7
Protein (g):	5.1
Sodium (mg):	171.6
Dietary Fiber (g):	1.2

White Cake

Yields two 9 inch layer cakes

INGREDIENTS:

3 cups all-purpose flour
1 ½ cups sugar
2 tsp. baking soda
2 tsp. baking powder
½ tsp. salt
½ cup plus 2 Tbsp.
   vegetable oil
1 Tbsp. vanilla
2 cups warm water

PREHEAT oven to 350° F.
COMBINE dry ingredients.
ADD remaining ingredients.
BEAT until smooth.
POUR into ungreased 9-inch cake pans.
BAKE 30 - 35 minutes.
COOL on rack.
FROST with desired frosting.
SERVE.

 No substitutions needed.

 Substitute 2 cups brown rice flour, ⅔ cup potato starch
& ⅓ cup tapioca flour for all-purpose flour.
Add 1 tsp. xanthan gum.

 No substitutions needed.

Nutritional Analysis:
(for base recipe)
Serving Size = ⅒ of cake

Calories (kcal):	375.9
Total Fat (g):	14.0
Saturated Fat (g):	1.9
Cholesterol (mg):	0
Carbohydrate (g):	59.0
Protein (g):	3.8
Sodium (mg):	468.1
Dietary Fiber (g):	1.0

Cookies

"American as Apple Pie" Cookies
Brownies
Chocolate Chip Cookies
Chocolate Dominos
Chocolate Wafers
Cream Cheese & Jelly Cookies
Gingerbread Kids
Ice Cream Cookie Baskets
Oatmeal Cookies
Peanut Butter Cookies
Snickerdoodles
Sugar Cookies

"American as Apple Pie" Cookies

Yields 5 dozen cookies

INGREDIENTS:

3 cups all-purpose flour

½ cup plus 2 Tbsp. sugar

½ cup margarine

½ cup vegetable shortening

6 - 8 Tbsp. ice water

2 tsp. cinnamon

2 ¼ cups "Apple Filling"
   (see recipe)

SIFT together flour & ¼ cup sugar.

CUT in margarine & shortening using a pastry blender or two knives until consistency of small beads.

ADD ice water, 1 Tbsp. at a time, to form stiff dough.

DIVIDE into three equal portions.

FREEZE in wax paper for 20 minutes.

COMBINE remaining sugar & cinnamon together & set aside.

TO FORM COOKIES

PREHEAT oven to 375° F.

ROLL OUT portion of dough, on lightly floured board, to form a rectangle ⅛ inch thick.

SPREAD ¾ cup pie filling, evenly, over dough.

SPRINKLE 2 Tbsp. sugar/cinnamon mixture over pie filling.

ROLL, jelly roll style, to form log.

CUT ½ inch slices, using serrated knife.

PLACE, cut side down, on greased cookie sheet.

REPEAT with remaining two portions of dough.

BAKE for 20 minutes or until crust is golden brown.

COOL on rack.

STORE in airtight container.

Use milk-free margarine.

Substitute ½ cup tapioca flour, ½ cup cornstarch, ¼ cup potato flour, 1 cup brown rice flour & 1 ½ tsp. xanthan gum for all-purpose flour. Substitute 1 egg, 2 tsp. apple cider vinegar & 2 Tbsp. ice water for water. Bake for 18 minutes.

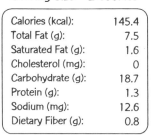

No substitutions needed.

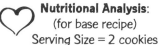

Nutritional Analysis:
   (for base recipe)
Serving Size = 2 cookies

Calories (kcal):	145.4
Total Fat (g):	7.5
Saturated Fat (g):	1.6
Cholesterol (mg):	0
Carbohydrate (g):	18.7
Protein (g):	1.3
Sodium (mg):	12.6
Dietary Fiber (g):	0.8

Brownies

Yields 16 brownies

INGREDIENTS:

3 oz. unsweetened chocolate

⅓ cup margarine

2 eggs

1 cup sugar

½ cup all-purpose flour

1 tsp. vanilla

PREHEAT oven to 350° F.

GREASE 8 x 8 inch pan & set aside.

MELT chocolate & margarine together on top of double boiler.

REMOVE from heat.

BEAT eggs with sugar until light & fluffy.

ADD chocolate mixture & blend until smooth.

MIX in flour & vanilla.

SPREAD batter into prepared pan.

BAKE for 20 - 25 minutes.

COOL in pan.

CUT & remove from pan.

SERVE.

Use milk-free margarine.

Substitute 6 Tbsp. brown rice flour & 2 Tbsp. tapioca flour for all-purpose flour.

Substitute 1 Tbsp. egg replacer mixed with ¼ cup water for eggs. Add 2 tsp. baking powder & 1 tsp. xanthan gum to all-purpose flour. Bake for approximately 30 minutes.

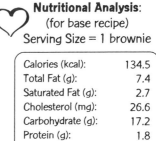

Nutritional Analysis:
(for base recipe)
Serving Size = 1 brownie

Calories (kcal):	134.5
Total Fat (g):	7.4
Saturated Fat (g):	2.7
Cholesterol (mg):	26.6
Carbohydrate (g):	17.2
Protein (g):	1.8
Sodium (mg):	53.2
Dietary Fiber (g):	0.9

Chocolate Chip Cookies

Yields 4 dozen cookies

INGREDIENTS:

½ cup margarine
¼ cup sugar
½ cup brown sugar
1 egg
½ tsp. vanilla
1 cup all-purpose flour
½ tsp. baking soda
1 cup chocolate chips

PREHEAT oven to 350° F.
CREAM together margarine, sugar & brown sugar until smooth.
ADD egg & vanilla & beat until absorbed.
STIR flour & baking soda into mixture to form dough.
ADD chocolate chips.
DROP by teaspoonfuls onto <u>ungreased</u> cookie sheet.
BAKE for 10 - 12 minutes.
COOL on rack.
SERVE.

 Use milk-free margarine & milk-free chocolate chips.

 Substitute ¼ cup soy flour & ¾ cup brown rice flour for all-purpose flour. Use gluten free chocolate.

 Omit egg. Drop by teaspoonfuls & flatten with fingers.

Nutritional Analysis:
(for base recipe)
Serving Size = 2 cookies

Calories (kcal):	117.7
Total Fat (g):	6.3
Saturated Fat (g):	2.1
Cholesterol (mg):	8.9
Carbohydrate (g):	15.3
Protein (g):	1.2
Sodium (mg):	82.6
Dietary Fiber (g):	0.6

Chocolate Dominos

Yields 5 dozen cookies

INGREDIENTS:

½ cup margarine, chilled
1 cup sugar
2 eggs
1 ½ tsp. vanilla
4 oz. unsweetened chocolate, melted

2 cups all-purpose flour
1 tsp. baking powder
½ tsp. salt
1 cup white chocolate chips

PREHEAT oven to 300° F.
CREAM sugar & margarine, until smooth.
BEAT in eggs, vanilla & chocolate.
MIX flour, baking powder & salt in separate bowl.
GRADUALLY ADD dry ingredients to sugar mixture, stirring until dough forms.
WRAP in wax paper.
REFRIGERATE for 20 minutes.
ROLL small portions of dough, on lightly floured surface, to ¼ inch thickness.
CUT into rectangles, 1 ½ inches x 3 inches.
MARK center of each "domino" across its width using back of knife. (Be careful not to press too hard.)
PRESS vanilla chips into cookies (point down) to form spots on "dominos".
BAKE on <u>ungreased</u> cookie sheet for 12 - 14 minutes (do not allow chips to brown).
REMOVE from oven & cool on cookie sheet for 2 minutes.
TRANSFER to rack & cool completely.
STORE in an airtight container.

Use milk-free margarine. Substitute 1 cup "Vanilla Frosting" (see recipe) for white chocolate chips. Pipe desired amount of domino "dots" on cookies.

Substitute 1¾ cups sweet rice flour & ½ cup tapioca flour for all-purpose flour.
Use gluten-free white chocolate chips.

Substitute 3 tsp. powdered egg replacer mixed with ¼ cup water for eggs.

Nutritional Analysis:
(for base recipe)
Serving Size = 2 cookies

Calories (kcal):	151.7
Total Fat (g):	7.7
Saturated Fat (g):	3.8
Cholesterol (mg):	14.2
Carbohydrate (g):	19.1
Protein (g):	1.7
Sodium (mg):	106.3
Dietary Fiber (g):	0.8

Chocolate Wafers

Yields 3 dozen cookies

INGREDIENTS:

¼ cup margarine

4 tsp. sugar

1 egg

2 Tbsp. unsweetened
cocoa powder

½ tsp. vanilla

½ tsp. peppermint flavoring

1 cup all-purpose flour

1 tsp. baking powder

¼ tsp. baking soda

2 Tbsp. water

COMBINE margarine, sugar, egg, cocoa, vanilla & peppermint.
BEAT until creamy.
ADD flour, baking powder, baking soda & water.
MIX well until dough forms.
SHAPE into ball.
DIVIDE in two parts & wrap in wax / plastic paper.
REFRIGERATE at least 2 hours (or freeze until firm).
PREHEAT oven to 350° F.
ROLL OUT on lightly floured surface to ⅛ inch thick.
CUT into 2 inch rounds.
BAKE on <u>ungreased</u> cookie sheet for 8 - 10 minutes.
COOL on rack.
SERVE.

 Recipe Variation: Use wafers to make cookie sandwiches with ice cream, peanut butter, jam, etc.

 Use milk-free margarine.

 Substitute 1 cup potato starch for all-purpose flour. Add 1 cup gluten-free chocolate chips or nuts to batter. Drop by spoonfuls (approx. 1 tsp.) onto <u>ungreased</u> cookie sheet.

 Substitute 2 Tbsp. water mixed with 1 ½ tsp. egg substitute for egg. Reduce baking time to 6 - 8 minutes. (This cookie can also be crumbled for topping or pie crust.)

 Nutritional Analysis:
(for base recipe)
Serving Size = 4 cookies

Calories (kcal):	114.7
Total Fat (g):	5.9
Saturated Fat (g):	1.2
Cholesterol (mg):	23.6
Carbohydrate (g):	13.3
Protein (g):	2.4
Sodium (mg):	164.9
Dietary Fiber (g):	0.8

Cream Cheese & Jelly Cookies

Yields 4 dozen cookies

INGREDIENTS:

¾ cup margarine, softened

8 oz. cream cheese

1 Tbsp. sugar

2 cups all-purpose flour

12 oz. jar preserves or spreadable fruit
(room temperature)

COMBINE margarine, cream cheese & sugar.

CREAM until fluffy.

MIX in flour to form a soft dough.

REFRIGERATE approximately 2 hours (or freeze until firm).

PREHEAT oven to 350° F.

ROLL OUT dough on floured surface to ⅛ inch thick, adding flour as needed.

CUT into 3 inch rounds.

PLACE ¼ tsp. preserves / spreadable fruit on each round.

FOLD in half.

CRIMP edges with a fork dipped in flour to seal.

PIERCE tops of cookies with sharp knife to vent.

BAKE on greased cookie sheet until lightly brown (about 10 minutes).

COOL on rack.

SERVE.

 Use tofu cream cheese & milk-free margarine.

 Substitute 1 cup plus 2 Tbsp. rice flour & ⅔ cup potato flour for all-purpose flour. Increase sugar to 2 Tbsp. Roll dough into balls (approximately ½ Tbsp. each). Place on greased cookie sheet. Make indentation with finger & fill with preserves. Increase baking time to 14 minutes.

 No substitutions needed.

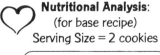 **Nutritional Analysis:**
(for base recipe)
Serving Size = 2 cookies

Calories (kcal):	154.8
Total Fat (g):	9.1
Saturated Fat (g):	3.2
Cholesterol (mg):	10.4
Carbohydrate (g):	16.6
Protein (g):	1.8
Sodium (mg):	94.6
Dietary Fiber (g):	0.3

Gingerbread Kids

Yields 3 dozen 4 inch cookies

INGREDIENTS:

¼ cup margarine
¼ cup brown sugar
¼ cup granulated sugar
½ cup molasses
3 ½ cups all-purpose flour
1 tsp. baking soda

1 tsp. cinnamon
½ tsp. ginger
½ tsp. salt
¼ cup water
"Gingerbread Icing" (see recipe)

PREHEAT oven to 350° F.

CREAM together margarine, brown sugar & sugar.

BLEND in molasses.

SIFT together flour, soda, cinnamon, ginger & salt.

ADD ⅓ margarine mixture.

ALTERNATE remaining margarine mixture with water until dough is formed & finish mixing with hands.

ROLL OUT small portions of dough to ¼ inch thickness on lightly greased board.

CUT into desired shapes & place on greased cookie sheet.

BAKE for 7 minutes.

COOL on rack.

FROST with "Gingerbread Icing".

SERVE.

 Recipe Variation: Decorate with raisins, nuts, dried fruit, pieces of candy or colored sugar before baking.

Use milk-free margarine.

Substitute 2 cups white rice flour with 1 cup soy flour & ¼ cup potato starch for all-purpose flour. Chill dough before rolling out. Bake for 7 - 9 minutes.

No substitutions needed.

 Nutritional Analysis:
(for base recipe-cookie only)
Serving Size = 1 cookie

Calories (kcal):	78.4
Total Fat (g):	1.4
Saturated Fat (g):	0.3
Cholesterol (mg):	0
Carbohydrate (g):	15.2
Protein (g):	1.3
Sodium (mg):	84.6
Dietary Fiber (g):	0.4

Ice Cream Cookie Baskets

Yields 12 baskets

INGREDIENTS:

3 egg whites
½ cup granulated sugar
⅓ cup light brown sugar
⅛ tsp. salt
½ cup melted margarine

½ cup all-purpose flour
6 Tbsp. finely ground almonds
¼ tsp. vanilla
3 pints ice cream

PREHEAT oven to 375° F.

MIX egg whites, granulated sugar, brown sugar & salt together until sugar dissolves.

STIR in remaining ingredients, one at a time, mixing completely.

DROP by heaping Tbsp. onto <u>ungreased</u> cookie sheet, two or three at a time, as cookies will spread considerably.

BAKE for 10 minutes or until edges are golden brown.

REMOVE from oven & working quickly, place each cookie over rim of 2 ½ inch wide glass to form "basket".

LET COOL for 1 minute.

REMOVE from glass & cool on rack.

FILL with scoop of ice cream.

SERVE.

★ cookies can be stored in airtight container for later use.

 Recipe Variation: Fill basket with fruit or pudding.

Use milk-free margarine & dairy-free frozen dessert.

Substitute 6 Tbsp. brown rice flour, 2 Tbsp. arrowroot & 1tsp. xanthan gum for all-purpose flour. Spread & flatten batter using back of spoon.

Substitute 4 ½ tsp. egg replacer mixed together with 6 Tbsp. water for egg whites.

Nutritional Analysis:
(for base recipe-basket only)
Serving Size = 1 basket

Calories (kcal):	155.7
Total Fat (g):	9.2
Saturated Fat (g):	1.6
Cholesterol (mg):	0
Carbohydrate (g):	17.0
Protein (g):	2.1
Sodium (mg):	128.5
Dietary Fiber (g):	0.5

Oatmeal Cookies

Yields 4 dozen cookies

INGREDIENTS:

½ cup granulated sugar
½ cup brown sugar
½ cup margarine
1 egg
1 ½ tsp. vanilla

1 cup all-purpose flour
½ tsp. baking soda
½ tsp. baking powder
¼ tsp. salt
1 ½ cups uncooked quick oats

PREHEAT oven to 350° F.

CREAM together sugar, brown sugar & margarine.

ADD egg & vanilla & set aside.

SIFT together flour, soda, baking powder & salt.

ADD to sugar mixture.

MIX in quick oats to form batter.

DROP by rounded teaspoons onto greased cookie sheet.

BAKE 10 - 12 minutes or until golden brown.

COOL on rack.

STORE in airtight container.

Use milk-free margarine.

Substitute ½ cup sweet rice flour & ½ cup white rice flour for all-purpose flour. Substitute 1 ½ cups coarsely crushed almonds for quick oats.

Substitute 2 Tbsp. water mixed together with 1 ½ tsp. egg replacer for egg.

Nutritional Analysis:
(for base recipe)
Serving Size = 2 cookies

Calories (kcal):	109.5
Total Fat (g):	4.4
Saturated Fat (g):	0.9
Cholesterol (mg):	8.9
Carbohydrate (g):	16.1
Protein (g):	1.6
Sodium (mg):	109.7
Dietary Fiber (g):	0.7

Peanut Butter Cookies

Yields 4 dozen cookies

INGREDIENTS:

1 cup creamy peanut butter (room temp.)
½ cup margarine, softened
½ cup sugar
½ cup brown sugar

1 egg
1 tsp. vanilla
½ tsp. baking soda
1 ½ cups all-purpose flour

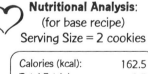

PREHEAT oven to 350° F.

CREAM peanut butter & margarine, until smooth.

ADD sugar & brown sugar, beat until smooth.

ADD egg & vanilla.

MIX in baking soda & flour to form dough.

ROLL or scoop dough into balls (Tbsp. size).

PLACE on greased cookie sheet.

PRESS cookies flat with bottom of glass or cross-wise with a fork.

BAKE 8 - 10 minutes or until golden brown.

COOL on rack.

SERVE.

 Recipe Variations: Drizzle ½ tsp. of melted chocolate on top of each cookie. You can also use chunky peanut butter.

 Use milk-free margarine.

 Substitute ¼ cup plus 2 Tbsp. soy flour & 1 cup plus 2 Tbsp. brown rice flour for all-purpose flour. Allow cookies to cool on cookie sheet for 2 minutes. Remove & cool on rack.

 Substitute 1 ½ tsp. egg replacer mixed with 2 Tbsp. water for eggs OR substitute ¼ cup Wonderslim® for margarine & 1 ½ Tbsp. water for egg. Allow cookies to cool on cookie sheet for 2 minutes. Remove & cool on rack.

Nutritional Analysis:
(for base recipe)
Serving Size = 2 cookies

Calories (kcal):	162.5
Total Fat (g):	9.5
Saturated Fat (g):	1.8
Cholesterol (mg):	8.9
Carbohydrate (g):	16.7
Protein (g):	3.8
Sodium (mg):	131.7
Dietary Fiber (g):	0.8

Snickerdoodles

Yields 3 dozen cookies

INGREDIENTS:

½ cup margarine
1 cup sugar
2 eggs
1 ½ tsp. vanilla

2 ½ cups all-purpose flour
1 tsp. baking powder
½ tsp. salt
cinnamon sugar ★

 cinnamon sugar: combine ½ cup sugar with 1 Tbsp. cinnamon.

PREHEAT oven to 350° F.

CREAM together margarine & sugar.

ADD eggs & vanilla & set aside.

MIX together flour, baking powder & salt in separate bowl.

GRADUALLY ADD to margarine mixture to form dough.

DROP by tablespoon into cinnamon sugar.

ROLL to coat.

PLACE on greased cookie sheet.

FLATTEN using bottom of glass dipped in cinnamon sugar.

BAKE 10 - 12 minutes.

REMOVE from cookie sheet.

COOL on rack.

SERVE.

Use milk-free margarine.

Substitute 1¾ cups sweet rice flour & ¾ cup soy flour for all-purpose flour.

Substitute ¼ cup water mixed together with 1 Tbsp. egg replacer for eggs.

Nutritional Analysis:
(for base recipe)
Serving Size = 2 cookies

Calories (kcal):	183.2
Total Fat (g):	5.8
Saturated Fat (g):	1.2
Cholesterol (mg):	23.6
Carbohydrate (g):	30.5
Protein (g):	2.5
Sodium (mg):	158.5
Dietary Fiber (g):	0.7

Sugar Cookies

Yields 5 dozen cookies

INGREDIENTS:

½ cup margarine, chilled
1 cup plus 2 Tbsp. sugar
2 eggs
1 ½ tsp. vanilla

2 ¼ cups all-purpose flour
1 tsp. baking powder
½ tsp. salt

PREHEAT oven to 350° F.

CREAM margarine & 1 cup sugar, until smooth.

ADD eggs & vanilla.

MIX flour, baking powder & salt in separate bowl & set aside.

GRADUALLY ADD dry ingredients to sugar mixture, stirring until dough forms.

WRAP in wax paper.

CHILL or freeze until firm.

ROLL small portions of dough on lightly floured surface to ¼ inch thickness.

CUT into 2 inch rounds.

SPRINKLE with remaining sugar.

BAKE on <u>ungreased</u> cookie sheet for 8 - 10 minutes.

COOL on rack.

SERVE.

 Use milk-free margarine.

 Substitute 1¾ cups sweet rice flour & ½ cup tapioca flour for all-purpose flour.

Substitute 3 tsp. powdered egg replacer mixed with ¼ cup water for eggs.

Nutritional Analysis:
(for base recipe)
Serving Size = 2 cookies

Calories (kcal):	95.8
Total Fat (g):	3.5
Saturated Fat (g):	0.7
Cholesterol (mg):	14.2
Carbohydrate (g):	14.8
Protein (g):	1.4
Sodium (mg):	95.0
Dietary Fiber (g):	0.3

Snacks

Cheese Sticks
Fossil Pretzels
Marshmallows
Sweet Rice Squares
Tortilla Chips

Cheese Sticks

Yields 2 dozen cheese sticks

INGREDIENTS:

¾ cup plus 2 Tbsp. all-purpose flour
¼ tsp. salt
1 tsp. baking powder
½ tsp. baking soda
1 ½ Tbsp. margarine, chilled

1 Tbsp. vegetable shortening
½ cup shredded cheddar cheese
⅓ cup water
½ Tbsp. melted margarine

PREHEAT oven to 425° F.
SIFT together flour, salt, baking powder & baking soda in bowl.
CUT in margarine & shortening using pastry blender
or two knives, until consistency of coarse corn meal.
ADD cheese.
FORM well in center of mixture.
POUR water into well & mix to form dough.
TURN dough out onto lightly floured board.
KNEAD for approximately 30 seconds.
TAKE ½ Tbsp. dough & roll to form stick.
REPEAT with remaining dough.
PLACE on ungreased cookie sheet.
BRUSH with melted margarine.
BAKE for 12 - 15 minutes, until golden brown & crispy.
SERVE.

Use milk-free cheese & margarine.

Substitute ½ cup brown rice flour & 6 Tbsp. potato starch flour for all-purpose flour. Increase baking powder to 2 tsp. Add 1tsp. xanthan gum to dry flour mixture. Substitute 5 Tbsp. club soda for water. Brush sticks with egg wash (1 beaten egg) in place of melted margarine.

No substitutions needed.

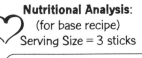

Nutritional Analysis:
(for base recipe)
Serving Size = 3 sticks

Calories (kcal):	117.6
Total Fat (g):	6.9
Saturated Fat (g):	2.5
Cholesterol (mg):	7.4
Carbohydrate (g):	10.6
Protein (g):	3.2
Sodium (mg):	289.9
Dietary Fiber (g):	0.4

Fossil Pretzels

Yields 12 pretzels

INGREDIENTS:

1 Tbsp. yeast
½ cup warm water
1 tsp. honey
1 tsp. salt
1⅓ cups all-purpose flour
1 egg, beaten
coarse salt

PREHEAT oven to 425° F.
DISSOLVE yeast in warm water.
ADD honey & salt.
MIX well.
STIR in flour & mix to form dough.
KNEAD dough, on a floured board, until smooth.
GRAB a piece of the dough & squeeze, making a fist.
PLACE on ungreased cookie sheet. Repeat until all dough is used.
BRUSH with beaten egg.
SPRINKLE with coarse salt.
BAKE at 425° F. for 10 - 12 minutes.
COOL on rack.
SERVE.

 Recipe Variation: Sprinkle pretzels with cinnamon, caraway seeds, sesame seeds, garlic & or herbs, etc.

 No substitutions needed.

Substitute 1 cup rice flour & ⅓ cup potato starch for all-purpose flour.

Brush pretzel with melted margarine or milk instead of egg.

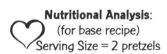 **Nutritional Analysis**:
(for base recipe)
Serving Size = 2 pretzels

Calories (kcal):	121.9
Total Fat (g):	1.2
Saturated Fat (g):	0.3
Cholesterol (mg):	35.4
Carbohydrate (g):	22.8
Protein (g):	4.7
Sodium (mg):	426.1
Dietary Fiber (g):	1.2

Marshmallows

Yields approx. 48 marshmallows

INGREDIENTS:

3 envelopes unflavored gelatin
½ cup cold water
1 ½ cups sugar
¼ tsp. salt

½ cup boiling water
1 tsp. vanilla
2 egg whites
powdered sugar

DUST one 8 x 10-inch square pan with powdered sugar.

SPRINKLE gelatin over cold water. Set aside.

COMBINE sugar, salt, & boiling water in a medium sauce pan & cook stirring constantly until sugar dissolves.

COOK over medium high heat until syrup reaches soft-crack stage* on a candy thermometer (280° F.)

REMOVE from heat.

ADD gelatin mixture & vanilla, stirring until gelatin dissolves.

COOL until syrup thickens.

BEAT egg whites in separate bowl until stiff.

POUR syrup into large mixing bowl.

BEAT syrup mixture for 5 - 8 minutes until fluffy.

FOLD in egg whites.

POUR mixture into prepared pan.

CHILL until set.

DUST top with powdered sugar.

REMOVE from pan.

CUT into cubes on board dusted with powdered sugar.

ROLL pieces in powdered sugar to coat entire marshmallow.

STORE in air tight container.

★ Soft Crack Candy Stage: Drop a small amount of mixture into a cup of cold water. Soft crack stage is when the mixture makes hard separate threads that bend when removed from the water.

No substitutions needed.

No substitutions needed.

Substitute 3 Tbsp. egg replacer mixed with 6 Tbsp. water for egg whites.

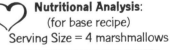

Nutritional Analysis:
(for base recipe)
Serving Size = 4 marshmallows

Calories (kcal):	115.3
Total Fat (g):	0
Saturated Fat (g):	0
Cholesterol (mg):	0
Carbohydrate (g):	27.3
Protein (g):	2.1
Sodium (mg):	62.1
Dietary Fiber (g):	0

Sweet Rice Squares

Yields 9 squares

INGREDIENTS:

1¾ cups puffed rice cereal
2 Tbsp. margarine
¼ tsp. vanilla
½ cup sugar

PREHEAT oven to 300° F.
WARM rice in oven for 5 minutes.
MELT margarine over medium heat.
ADD vanilla & sugar
STIR constantly until sugar has dissolved & mixture thickens.
PLACE rice in greased 8 x 8 inch pan.
POUR syrup over rice.
MIX quickly.
PRESS evenly into bottom of pan.
REFRIGERATE until cool.
CUT into squares.
SERVE.

 Recipe Variation: Mix in raisins, nuts, chocolate chips, cocoa, etc.

 Use milk-free margarine.

 No substitutions needed.

 No substitutions needed.

Nutritional Analysis:
(for base recipe)
Serving Size = 1 oz. (1 square)

Calories (kcal):	77.2
Total Fat (g):	2.5
Saturated Fat (g):	0.5
Cholesterol (mg):	0
Carbohydrate (g):	13.7
Protein (g):	0.2
Sodium (mg):	29.8
Dietary Fiber (g):	0.1

Tortilla Chips

Yields 4 dozen chips

INGREDIENTS:

12 "Tortillas" (see recipe)
vegetable oil for frying
salt to taste

CUT tortillas into quarters.
HEAT 1-inch vegetable oil in skillet.
DROP tortilla pieces in oil & fry until golden brown.
REMOVE with slotted spoon.
PLACE chips in paper bag.
ADD salt to taste.
SHAKE bag to drain oil.
SERVE or store in airtight container (for up to 2 weeks).

 Recipe Variation: Chips can be placed on <u>ungreased</u> cookie sheet
& baked for 10 - 12 minutes at 375° F.

 No substitutions needed.

No substitutions needed.

No substitutions needed.

 Nutritional Analysis:
(for base recipe)
Serving Size = 1oz. (approx. 6 chips)

Calories (kcal):	212.0
Total Fat (g):	2.7
Saturated Fat (g):	0.4
Cholesterol (mg):	0
Carbohydrate (g):	43.2
Protein (g):	5.3
Sodium (mg):	168.9
Dietary Fiber (g):	5.4

Icings & Glazes

Chocolate Glaze
Chocolate Icing
Gingerbread Icing
Vanilla Icing

Chocolate Glaze

Yields 1 cup

INGREDIENTS:

4 oz. semi-sweet chocolate chips
¼ cup water
¼ cup margarine
3 Tbsp. confectioners sugar

MELT chocolate & water in top of double boiler.
REMOVE from heat.
ADD margarine & confectioners sugar.
WHISK until smooth.
COOL until slightly thickened (glaze can be reheated
       if it becomes too thick)
USE with you favorite dessert recipe.

Use dairy-free chocolate chips & milk-free margarine.

Use gluten-free chocolate.

No substitutions needed.

Nutritional Analysis:
(for base recipe)
Serving Size = 2 tsp.

Calories (kcal):	43.4
Total Fat (g):	3.3
Saturated Fat (g):	1.2
Cholesterol (mg):	0
Carbohydrate (g):	4.0
Protein (g):	0.2
Sodium (mg):	22.8
Dietary Fiber (g):	0.3

Chocolate Icing

Yields 2 cups

INGREDIENTS:

4 cups confectioners sugar
½ cup margarine, softened
¼ cup milk
3 tsp. vanilla
½ cup unsweetened cocoa

CREAM sugar & margarine together.
ADD milk, vanilla & cocoa.
BEAT until smooth.
USE with your favorite cake recipe.

Use milk-free margarine & dairy-free milk substitute.

No substitutions needed.

No substitutions needed.

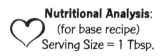

Nutritional Analysis:
(for base recipe)
Serving Size = 1 Tbsp.

Calories (kcal):	87.2
Total Fat (g):	3.1
Saturated Fat (g):	0.7
Cholesterol (mg):	0.3
Carbohydrate (g):	15.8
Protein (g):	0.4
Sodium (mg):	34.7
Dietary Fiber (g):	0.5

Gingerbread Icing

Yields 1 cup

INGREDIENTS:

2 cups confectioners sugar
¼ cup water
food coloring (optional)

MIX confectioners sugar with water until smooth.
ADD desired amount of food coloring.
DECORATE cookies.

No substitutions needed.

No substitutions needed.

No substitutions needed.

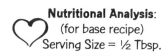

Nutritional Analysis:
(for base recipe)
Serving Size = ½ Tbsp.

Calories (kcal):	29.2
Total Fat (g):	0
Saturated Fat (g):	0
Cholesterol (mg):	0
Carbohydrate (g):	7.5
Protein (g):	0
Sodium (mg):	0.1
Dietary Fiber (g):	0

Vanilla Icing

Yields 2 cups

INGREDIENTS:

4 cups confectioners sugar
½ cup margarine, softened
¼ cup milk
3 tsp. vanilla

CREAM sugar & margarine together.
ADD milk & vanilla.
BEAT until smooth.
USE with your favorite cake recipe.

Use milk-free margarine & dairy-free milk substitute.

No substitutions needed.

No substitutions needed.

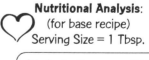

Nutritional Analysis:
(for base recipe)
Serving Size = 1 Tbsp.

Calories (kcal):	86.1
Total Fat (g):	2.9
Saturated Fat (g):	0.6
Cholesterol (mg):	0.3
Carbohydrate (g):	15.1
Protein (g):	0.1
Sodium (mg):	34.4
Dietary Fiber (g):	0

Drinks

Banana Smoothie

Orange Peach Cooler

Peach Orange Smoothie

Strawberry Smoothie

Watermelon Smoothie

Banana Smoothie

Yields 3 servings

INGREDIENTS:
½ cup plain yogurt
1 cup vanilla ice cream
1 cup mashed banana

PUREE ingredients until smooth.
POUR into tall glasses.
SERVE.

 Serving Suggestion: Pour smoothie into paper cups or ice cube trays with craft sticks & freeze to make popsicles!

 Substitute 1 cup vanilla dairy-free frozen dessert for ice cream & ½ cup silken tofu for yogurt. Add ½ cup water.

No substitutions needed.

No substitutions needed.

Nutritional Analysis:
(for base recipe)
Serving Size = 8 oz.

Calories (kcal):	182.5
Total Fat (g):	6.5
Saturated Fat (g):	4.0
Cholesterol (mg):	24.6
Carbohydrate (g):	29.9
Protein (g):	3.7
Sodium (mg):	54.9
Dietary Fiber (g):	1.8

Orange Peach Cooler

Yields 3 servings

INGREDIENTS:
4 medium peaches, very ripe
1 cup orange juice
1 cup milk
½ tsp. vanilla

PEEL peaches & cut into chunks.
PUREE peaches & orange juice together in blender or food processor until smooth.
FREEZE until firm.
REMOVE from freezer.
PUREE until smooth.
RE-FREEZE until firm.
PUT in blender with milk & vanilla.
BLEND until smooth.
POUR into glass.
SERVE.

Use milk substitute.

No substitutions needed.

No substitutions needed.

Nutritional Analysis:
(for base recipe)
Serving Size = 8 oz.

Calories (kcal):	147.0
Total Fat (g):	3.3
Saturated Fat (g):	1.9
Cholesterol (mg):	11.6
Carbohydrate (g):	26.7
Protein (g):	4.3
Sodium (mg):	40.6
Dietary Fiber (g):	2.8

Peach Orange Smoothie

Yields 4 servings

INGREDIENTS:

6 medium peaches, very ripe
1 cup orange juice
½ cup plain yogurt
1 cup vanilla ice cream

PEEL peaches & cut into chunks.
PUREE peaches & orange juice together in blender or food processor until smooth.
ADD remaining ingredients.
BLEND until smooth.
POUR into glass.
SERVE.

Use dairy-free frozen dessert for ice cream & substitute
½ cup silken tofu for yogurt.

No substitutions needed.

No substitutions needed.

Nutritional Analysis:
(for base recipe)
Serving Size = 8 oz.

Calories (kcal):	175.7
Total Fat (g):	4.9
Saturated Fat (g):	2.9
Cholesterol (mg):	18.4
Carbohydrate (g):	31.8
Protein (g):	3.7
Sodium (mg):	41.2
Dietary Fiber (g):	3.1

Strawberry Smoothie

Yields 3 servings

INGREDIENTS:
½ cup plain yogurt
1 cup vanilla ice cream
2 cups strawberries
2 tsp. sugar

PUREE ingredients until smooth.
POUR into tall glasses.
SERVE.

 Serving Suggestion: Pour smoothie into paper cups or ice cube trays with craft sticks & freeze to make popsicles!

Use dairy-free frozen dessert for ice cream & substitute ½ cup silken tofu for yogurt.

No substitutions needed.

No substitutions needed.

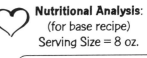 **Nutritional Analysis**:
(for base recipe)
Serving Size = 8 oz.

Calories (kcal):	153.2
Total Fat (g):	6.5
Saturated Fat (g):	3.9
Cholesterol (mg):	24.6
Carbohydrate (g):	21.8
Protein (g):	3.5
Sodium (mg):	55.1
Dietary Fiber (g):	2.2

Watermelon Smoothie

Yields 4 servings

INGREDIENTS:

2 cups diced watermelon,
   firmly packed
½ cup plain yogurt
1 cup vanilla ice cream

PUREE ingredients until smooth.
POUR into tall glasses.
SERVE.

Serving Suggestion: Pour smoothie into paper cups or
ice cube trays with craft sticks & freeze to make popsicles!

Use dairy-free frozen dessert for ice cream &
substitute ½ cup silken tofu for yogurt.

No substitutions needed.

No substitutions needed.

Nutritional Analysis:
(for base recipe)
Serving Size = 8 oz.

Calories (kcal):	110.7
Total Fat (g):	5.0
Saturated Fat (g):	2.9
Cholesterol (mg):	18.4
Carbohydrate (g):	15.0
Protein (g):	2.7
Sodium (mg):	42.2
Dietary Fiber (g):	0.4

Resources

Dairy-Free Resources

Allergy and Asthma Network	Association
American Academy of Allergy and Immunology	Association
American Academy of Pediatrics	Association
American Natural Snacks	Soy cheeses
Asthma and Allergy Foundation of America	Association
Blue Diamond Growers	Almond milk
Cemac Foods	Tofu cheeses
Child Health Alert	Newsletter
Cloud Nine, Inc.	"Tropical Source" Dairy-free chocolate
Eden Foods, Inc.	Dairy-free products, alternative milk products
Food Allergy Network	Association & Newsletter
Hain Food Group Inc.,	Dairy-free products
Health Valley Foods, Inc.,	Soy milk
Imagine Foods	"Rice Dream" dairy-free milk products & frozen desserts
International Food Allergy Association	Association
McNeil Consumer Products Co.	"Lactaid" lactose-free dairy products

Medic Alert Foundation International	Allergy ID bracelets & wallet cards
Nasoya Foods, Inc.,	Dairy-free spreads
Natural Food Technologies	"Wonderslim" butter substitute
The Newsletter: For People With Lactose Intolerance & Milk Allergy	Newsletter
Pacific Foods of Oregon, Inc.,	Alternative dairy beverages
Rich Products Corporation	Non-dairy creamer & whipped cream
Soyco Foods	Soy cheeses
Sweet Nothings	Dairy-free frozen desserts
U.S. Department of Agriculture Food & Nutrition Service	Government Agency
U.S. Department of Health & Human Services	Government Agency
U.S. Food & Drug Administration	Government Agency
Vitasoy USA Inc.,	Soy beverages
Westbrae Natural Foods, Inc.,	Soy beverages
Wholesome & Hearty Foods	Almond milk & cheeses

156

Gluten-free Resources

Allergy and Asthma Network	Association
Allergy Resources, Inc.,	Gluten-free baking products
American Academy of Allergy and Immunology	Association
American Academy of Pediatrics	Association
American Celiac Society	Association
Arrowhead Mills	Gluten-free baking mixes & alternative flours
Asthma & Allergy Foundation of America	Association
Belo Foods, Inc.,	Gluten-free English muffins
Bob's Red Mill	Alternative flours
Celiac Disease Foundation	Association
Celiac Sprue Association	Association
Cemac Foods	Gluten-free pasta
Child Health Alert	Newsletter
Cloud Nine, Inc.,	"Tropical Source" gluten-free chocolate
Dietary Specialties, Inc.,	Mail order gluten-free products
Eden Foods, Inc.,	Gluten-free pasta, vinegar & other products
Ener-G Foods, Inc.	Gluten-free baking mixes, alternative flours & other products
Food Allergy Network	Association & Newsletter
Food For Life Baking Company	Gluten-free bread

Gluten-Free Bounty	Mail order gluten-free products
Gluten-Free Living	Newsletter
The Gluten-Free Pantry, Inc.,	Gluten-free baking mixes & baking products
Hain Food Group, Inc.,	Gluten-free products
Hodgson Mill	Gluten-free flours
International Food Allergy Association	Association
Life Source Natural Foods, Inc.,	"Pastariso" rice pasta
Medic Alert Foundation International	Allergy ID bracelets & wallet cards
Menu Direct Corporation	Mail order prepared meals
Miss Robens	Mail order gluten-free mixes & baking products
Mrs. Leeper's, Inc.,	Corn pasta
Pamela's Products, Inc.,	Gluten-free baking mixes & cookies
Quinoa Corporation	Quinoa pasta, cereals & flour
Shiloh Farms	Alternative flours
Spectrum Naturals, Inc.,	Rice vinegar
Tad Enterprises	Gluten-free mixes, flours & products
U.S. Department of Agriculture, Food & Nutrition Service	Government Agency
U.S. Department of Health & Human Services	Government Agency
U.S. Food & Drug Administration	Government Agency
Westbrae Natural Foods, Inc.,	Corn pasta

Egg-free Resources

Allergy and Asthma Network	Association
American Academy of Allergy and Immunology	Association
American Academy of Pediatrics	Association
Arrowhead Mills	Egg-free baking mixes
Asthma & Allergy Foundation of America	Association
Child Health Alert	Newsletter
Ener-G Foods, Inc.,	"Egg Replacer", egg-free baking mixes & products
Food Allergy Network	Association & Newsletter
Hain Food Group, Inc.,	Egg-free mayonnaise
International Food Allergy Association	Association
Medic Alert Foundation International	Allergy ID bracelets & wallet cards
Nasoya Foods Inc.,	Egg-free mayonnaise & sandwich spreads
Natural Food Technologies	"Wonderslim" Egg substitute
U.S. Department of Agriculture, Food & Nutrition Service	Government Agency
U.S. Department of Health & Human Services	Government Agency
U.S. Food & Drug Administration	Government Agency

Resource Directory

Allergy and Asthma Network
3554 Chain Bridge Road. Suite 200
Fairfax, VA 22030
800-878-4403

Allergy Resources, Inc.
P.O. Box 888
Palmer Lake, CO 80133
800-873-3529

American Academy of Allergy and Immunology
611 East Wells Street
Milwaukee, WI 53202
414-272-6071

American Academy of Pediatrics
141 Northwest Point Blvd.
P.O. Box 927
Elk Grove Village, IL 60009-0927
800-433-9016

American Celiac Society
58 Musano Court
West Orange, NJ 07052
201-325-8837

American Natural Snacks
P.O. Box 1067
St. Augustine, FL 32085-1067
904-825-2057
904-825-2024 (fax)

Arrowhead Mills
P.O. Box 2059
Hereford, TX 79045-2059
806-364-0730
806-364-8242 (fax)

Asthma & Allergy Foundation of America
1717 Massachusetts Avenue NW, Suite 305
Washington, D.C. 20036
800-7-ASTHMA

Belo Foods, Inc.
Waterbury, CT
203-756-1100

Blue Diamond Growers
1802 C Street
Sacramento, CA 95814
916-442-0771

Bob's Red Mill
Natural Foods, Inc.
Milwaukee, OR 97222

Celiac Disease Foundation
11315 Dona Lola Drive
P.O. Box 1265
Studio City, CA 91614-0265
213-654-4085

The Celiac Sprue Association
P.O. Box 31700
Omaha, NE 68103-0700
402-558-0600

Cemac Foods
1821 East Sedgley Avenue
Philadelphia, PA 19124
800-724-0179
215-533-8993 (fax)

Child Health Alert
P.O. Box 610228
Newton Highlands, MA 02161
617-239-1762

Cloud Nine Inc.
Hoboken, NJ 07030

Dietary Specialties Inc.
P.O. Box 227
Rochester, NY 14601-0227
800-544-0099
716-232-6168 (fax)

Eden Foods, Inc.
701 Tecumseh Road
Clinton, MI 49236
800-248-0301
517-456-6075 (fax)

Ener-G Foods, Inc.
5960 First Avenue South
Seattle, WA 98124-5787
800-331-5222
206-764-3398 (fax)

The Food Allergy Network
10400 Eaton Place, Suite 107
Fairfax, VA 22030-2208
703-691-3179
703-691-2713 (fax)

Food for Life Baking Company
P.O. Box 1434
Corona, CA 91718-1434

Gluten-Free Bounty
7305 Woodbine Avenue, Suite 268
Markham, ONT Canada L3R3V7

Gluten-Free Living
P.O. Box 105
Hastings-On-Hudson, NY 10706

The Gluten-Free Pantry, Inc.
P.O. Box 881
Glastonbury, CT 06033
860-633-3826
860-633-6853 (fax)

Gluten Intolerance Group of North America
P.O. 23053
Seattle, WA 98102-0353
206-325-6980

Hain Food Group, Inc.
50 Charles Lindbergh Blvd.
Uniondale, NY 11553
800-434-HAIN

Health Valley Foods, Inc.
700 Union Street
Montebello, CA 90604

Hodgson Mill Inc.
1203 Niccum Avenue
Suite 1
Effingham, IL 62401
800-525-0177

Imagine Foods
350 Cambridge Avenue
Palo Alto, CA 94306
415-327-1444
415-327-1459 (fax)

International Food Allergy Association
822 South Maple Avenue
Oak Park, IL 60304
708-386-9090

Life Source Natural Foods, Inc.
1773 Bayley Street
Pickering, ONT Canada L1W2Y7
905-831-5433
905-831-4333 (fax)

McNeil Consumer Products Co.
7050 Camp Hill Road
Fort Washington, PA 19034-2299
215-233-7000

Medic Alert Foundation International
P.O. Box 1009
Turlock, CA 95381-1009
800-432-5378

Menu Direct Corporation
865 Centennial Avenue
Piscataway, NJ 08854
888-MENU123

Miss Robens
P.O. Box 1434
Frederick, MD 21702
800-891-0083
301-631-5954 (fax)

Mrs. Leeper's Inc.
Poway, CA 92064

Nasoya Foods Inc.
Ayer, MA 01432
800-229-TOFU

Natural Food Technologies
14241 East Firestone Blvd.
La Mirada, CA 90638
310-802-0102
310-802-1131 (fax)

The Newsletter: For People With
Lactose Intolerance and Milk Allergy
P.O. Box 3129
Ann Arbor, MI 48106-3129
313-572-9134

Pacific Foods of Oregon, Inc.
Tualatin, OR 97062
503-692-9666

Pamela's Products, Inc.
364 Littlefield Avenue
South San Francisco, CA 94080
415-952-4546
415-742-6643 (fax)

Quinoa Corp.
P.O. Box 1039
Torrance, CA 90505
310-530-8666
310-530-8764 (fax)

Rich Products Corp.
1150 Niagara Street
Buffalo, NY 14240

Shiloh Farms
P.O. Box 97
Sulpha Springs, AR 72768
501-298-3297

Soyco Foods
2441 Viscount Row
Orlando, FL 32809

Spectrum Naturals, Inc.
133 Copeland Street
Petaluma, CA 94952

Sweet Nothings
Division of Turtle Mountain Inc.
P.O. Box 70
Junction City, OR 97448

Tad Enterprises
9356 Pleasant
Tinley Park, IL 60477
708-429-2101

U.S. Department of Agriculture
Food and Nutrition Service
Room 304
10301 Baltimore Blvd.
Beltsville, MD 20705-2351

U.S. Department of Health and Human Services
Public Health Service
Health Resources and Services Administration
Maternal and Child Health Bureau
Washington D.C. 20857

U.S. Food and Drug Administration
5600 Fisher's Lane
Bathesda, MD 20857

Vitasoy USA, Inc.
P.O. Box 2012
S. San Francisco, CA 94083

Westbrae Natural Foods, Inc.
Carson, CA 90746
310-886-8200

Wholesome & Hearty Foods
975 S.E. Sandy Blvd.
Portland, OR 97214
503-238-0109
503-232-6485 (fax)

Bibliography & Endnotes

Bibliography

Adelman, Todd and Behrend, Jodi. "I'm Having a Reaction to my Child's Food Allergies." Tuesday's Child, vol. 2(5) (October, 1998), pp. 31-34.

Adelman, Todd and Behrend, Jodi. "Living with Kid's Food Allergies." Queens Parent, vol. 3(11) (February, 1998), pp. 25-27.

Adelman, Todd and Behrend, Jodi. "Don't Eat That." PARENTGUIDE, vol. 15(11) (November, 1997),p.34.

Allergy Information Association. The Food Allergy Cookbook. New York: St Martin's Press, 1983.

Barrett, Patricia and Dalton, Rosemary. The Kids Cookbook. Yum I Eat It! California:Nitty Gritty Books, 1973.

Catassi, C., Ratsch, I-M., Fabrani, E., Rossini, M., Bordicchia, F., Candela, F., Coppa,   G.V., & Giorg, P.L.. "Celiac disease in the year 2000; exploring the iceberg." The Lancet. vol. 343, (1994), p. 200.

Dong, Faye M.. All About Food Allergy. Philadelphia: George F. Stickley Co., 1984.

Gioannini, Marilyn. The Complete Food Allergy Cookbook. California: Prima Publishing, 1996.

Hagman, Bette. More From the Gluten-Free Gourmet. New York: Henry Holt and Company, Inc., 1990.

Harris, Mary and Nachsin, Wilma. "My Kid's Allergic to Everything" Dessert Cookbook. Chicago: Chicago Review Press Inc., 1996.

Hurt Jones, Marjorie. The Allergy Self-Help Cookbook. New York: Wings Books,1984.

Jacobson, Michael and Hill, Laura. Kitchen Fun For Kids. New York: Henry Holt and Company, Inc., 1991.

Kidder, Beth. The Milk-Free Kitchen. New York: Henry Holt and Company, Inc., 1991.

Kjellman, N.-I.. "Epidemiology of Food Allergy. In Eberhardt Schmidt (Ed.),. Food Allergy: Nestle Nutrition Workshop Series,. New York: Vevey/Raven Press, Ltd. (1988), pp.119-123.

Meizel, Janet. *Your Food-Allergic Child: A Parent's Guide.* Massachusetts: Mills & Sanderson, 1988.

Meyer, Elisa. *Feeding Your Allergic Child.* New York: St. Martin's Press, 1997.

Muñoz-Furlong, Anne. *The Food Allergy News Cookbook.* Virginia: The Food Allergy Network, 1992.

Potts, Phyllis. *Still Going Against the Grain.* Oregon: Central Point Publishing, 1994.

"Problems with Milk: Allergy vs. Intolerance." *Child Health Alert.* Vol. 11 (4), (June 1993).

Reno, Liz and Devrais, Joanna. *Allergy Free Eating.* California: Celestial Arts Publishing, 1995.

Rhude Yoder, Eileen. *Allergy-Free Cooking.* New York: Addison-Wesley Publishing Company, 1987.

Rombauer, Erma S. and Rombauer Becker, Marion. *Joy Of Cooking.* Indiana: The Bobs-Merrill Company, Inc., 1967.

Rudoff, Carol. *The Allergy Cookie Jar.* California: Prologue Publications, 1985.

Shattuck, Ruth R. *The Allergy Cookbook.* New York: Penguin Books, Ltd., 1884.

Somer, E.. *Women's Sports and Fitness,* vol.15 (7), (October,1993), p.19.

Somerville, Sylvia. "Food-Allergy Awareness: Decreasing the danger in dining out." *Restaurant USA,* vol.15 (10) (November 1995), pp.35-38.

Springen, K.. *Vegetarian Times,* vol. 200, (April,1994), p.98.

Sunset Books, Editors. *Cookies: Step-By-Step Techniques.* California: Lane PublishingCompany, 1985.

Tracy, Lisa. *KIDFOOD.* New York: Dell Publishing, 1979.

United States Department of Agriculture. "The Food Guide Pyramid." *Home and Garden Bulletin Number 252,* (October, 1996), pp. 1-29.

Zukin, Jane. *Raising Your Child Without Milk.* California: Prima Publishing, 1996.

Endnotes

I *Problems with Milk: Allergy vs. Intolerance.* (1993, June). Child Health Alert. 11 (4).

II *Springen, K.* (1994, April). Vegetarian Times, 200 , 98.

III *Somer, E.* (1993, October). Women's Sports and Fitness, 15 (7), 19.

IV *Dong, F. M.* (1984). All About Food Allergy. George F. Stickley Company.

V *Catassi, C., Ratsch, I-M., Fabrani, E., Rossini, M., Bordicchia, F., Candela, F., Coppa, G.V., & Giorg, P.L.* (1994). Celiac disease in the year 2000; exploring the iceberg. The Lancet. 343, 200.

VI *Kjellman, N.-I.* (1988). Epidemiology of Food Allergy. In Eberhardt Schmidt (Ed.),Food Allergy: Nestle Nutrition Workshop Series, (pp. 119-123). New York: Vevey/Raven Press, Ltd.

The nutritional analysis for our recipes was calculated using the following software: Nutrient Standard Menu Planning version 4.1 (c) 1995; SNAP Systems, Inc.

Graphic design and layout for
"Special Foods for Special Kids"
by:

Recipe Index

Here's how to order additional copies of

Special Foods for Special Kids

By Todd Adelman & Jodi Behrend

Please send $16.95 per copy, plus $4.00 shipping and handling for a total of $20.95. In New York State please add appropriate sales tax. For each additional copy to the same address, add $1.50 for shipping. Send check or money order payable to:

Cooking Creative, LLC
P.O. Box 234403
Great Neck, NY 11023

For information on quantity discounts please contact us.

Your name (please print)_____

Address to send book(s)_____

_____

Number of copies ordered:_____ Amount: _____